Praise for *College Without High School*

Words fail me. This is the most inspiring, convincing, and practical case for self-directed learning that I've seen in many years. Mr. Boles draws on time management principles from the business world and on his own adventure-packed youth to map out a brilliantly simple way that people can live life to the fullest while also preparing masterfully for admission to college. If you believe, as I do, that our time on earth is a grand gift not to be squandered, then buy this book for all the teenagers you love, and watch as all manner of quests, discoveries, inventions, and miracles emerge.

— Grace Llewellyn, author of *The Teenage Liberation Handbook: how to quit school and get a real life and education* and *Real Lives: Eleven Teenagers Who Don't Go to School Tell Their Own Stories*

This splendid book is intended as a step-by-step guide, but can be read with profit by anyone interested in moral philosophy. Exceptionally clear, insightful, and lively, it will take its place as the definitive work on the subject.

— John Taylor Gatto, author of *Dumbing Us Down*, *The Underground History of American Education*, and *Weapons of Mass Instruction*

Boles offers an antidote to the over-scheduled, grade-driven, and sadly uncreative existence of most high-schoolers today. It's time for teens to take control of their own education. Yes, they must learn the basics. Absolutely. But as Boles explains, self-motivated teens can cover those topics efficiently and free up more of their time for further learning. This book is a crucial guide for students and parents interested in replacing the old carrot and stick that's at the heart of today's education system with intrinsic motivation—self-directedness and autonomy that leads to real learning and growth.

— Daniel H. Pink, author of *A Whole New Mind* ›nd *The Adventures Of Johnny Bunko*

Blake Boles has found the solution for those students who find regular high school oppressive. Outstanding advice! His book is absolutely right on about the many options for success for students who have a little different approach to life and study.

— Donald Asher, author of *Cool Colleges For the Hyper-Intelligent, Self-Directed, Late Blooming, and Just Plain Different*

College Without High School is an excellent update to the groundwork provided by John Holt, the Colfaxes, Grace Llewellyn, and other unschoolers. I found it engaging and filled with concrete understanding and useful suggestions for Self Directed Learners of all ages, in or out of school.

— Cafi Cohen, author of *And What About College?: How homeschooling leads to admissions to the best colleges and universities*

College Without High School is a fantastic resource for homeschoolers who want to stand out from the rest of the college admissions pack. However, especially for unschoolers and other eclectic learners, it is also an inspirational description for how adventurous self-directed learning can lead to college admission. This is an entertaining workbook, how-to manual, and educational philosophy text that will help teenagers and their families figure out how to get into college without a conventional high school degree.

— Patrick Farenga, co-author of *Teach Your Own: The John Holt Book of Homeschooling*

Blake Boles shares what homeschoolers have known for decades: teens are thriving everywhere without attending school! Blake will inspire you to seize the day and live well now, with every bit of confidence that the doors to college will be wide open to you. I am thrilled to have another messenger trumpet the truth that school is optional. I recommend all parents and educators to acquaint themselves with this information.

— Kenneth Danford, co-founder and executive director of North Star: Self-Directed Learning for Teens

COLLEGE
WITHOUT
HIGH
SCHOOL

A teenager's guide to skipping high school and going to college

BLAKE BOLES

NEW SOCIETY PUBLISHERS

CATALOGING IN PUBLICATION DATA:

A catalog record for this publication is available
from the National Library of Canada.

Cover design by Diane McIntosh.

Printed in Canada by Friesens.
First printing July 2009.

Paperback ISBN: 978-0-86571-655-1

Inquiries regarding requests to reprint all or part of *College Without High School* should be addressed to New Society Publishers at the address below.

To order directly from the publishers, please call toll-free (North America)
1-800-567-6772, or order online at www.newsociety.com

Any other inquiries can be directed by mail to:

New Society Publishers
P.O. Box 189, Gabriola Island, BC V0R 1X0, Canada
(250) 247-9737

New Society Publishers' mission is to publish books that contribute in fundamental ways to building an ecologically sustainable and just society, and to do so with the least possible impact on the environment, in a manner that models this vision. We are committed to doing this not just through education, but through action. This book is one step toward ending global deforestation and climate change. It is printed on Forest Stewardship Council-certified acid-free paper that is **100% post-consumer recycled** (100% old growth forest-free), processed chlorine free, and printed with vegetable-based, low-VOC inks, with covers produced using FSC-certified stock. Additionally, New Society purchases carbon offsets based on an annual audit, operating with a carbon-neutral footprint. For further information, or to browse our full list of books and purchase securely, visit our website at: www.newsociety.com

NEW SOCIETY PUBLISHERS
www.newsociety.com

For Ross, Liza, Cooper, Olivia and Ben

Contents

Premises and Promises

Is a Life of Teenage Adventure for You?

Most high schoolers never consider the possibility of life outside the classroom. But that life exists, and it's lived every day by a growing number of non-traditional students: unschoolers.

For an unschooler, each day is a chance for a new adventure. You might find one volunteering on an organic farm in France, bike-riding across state lines with friends, taking pulses as an emergency room intern, making phone calls to favorite authors, crashing a college physics lecture, blogging about graphic design or running a tutoring business. These teens pursue their dreams on a daily basis—and they still get into college.

Emerie Snyder entered New York University's revered Tisch School of Arts without a day of high school on her transcript. Andy Pearson never went to any school but began part-time college courses at the University of Michigan at age 16 (and soon became a full-time student). Charlotte Wagoner studies International Business at Rockhurst, and Shannon Lee Clair writes plays at Princeton—each without four years of high school to their names. Unschooled teens have gained admission to virtually every competitive college in the US. These unschoolers aren't Einstein-like geniuses. They're normal teens who, unsatisfied with school's plan for their future, chose to get an education on their own terms. You can make this choice, too.

Ask yourself if the following premises make sense. If they do, then you might be a closet unschooler, and a life of teenage adventure awaits you.

School and Education are *Not* the Same Thing

School is a place where people go; education is gaining the confidence to follow your dreams. You can succeed in life without school, but you'll fail terribly without an education.

You Can Learn More by Going to School Less

Learning is driven by interest and relevancy, not threats and bribery. If biology fascinates you, you'll learn it quickly. If computer science is relevant to your dreams, then you'll focus on it. The motivational machinery used by schools — constant testing, grading and comparison — discourages learning in curious minds.

Getting Into a Top College Does Not Require Full-Time High School

Getting into a top college *does* require proving that you can handle rigorous academics, structured classroom learning and the other skills that college requires. Unschoolers find alternative paths to proving these points: they enroll in community college classes, use SAT and AP tests to demonstrate proficiency or highlight the intellectual challenges of their self-directed projects (among dozens of other options).

Leaving School Does Not Lock You Into a Fast Food Career

Life is not a pyramid with doctors, lawyers and professors on the top, McDonald's cashiers at the bottom and school the only ladder between. The US is home to countless intelligent and financially successful adults who left the traditional school path. Choosing to leave school is an entrepreneurial move, not a cop-out.

Life Doesn't Have to Wait Until Age 18

You're not legally an adult until age 18, but that doesn't mean you have to let school control your life until then. Thirteen-year-old Native Americans patrolled their villages on horseback, and 16-year-old Robin Lee Graham sailed around the world on his boat, *Dove*. You're mentally and physically capable of making important decisions for yourself. If high school feels like a waste of time better spent elsewhere, go elsewhere. Leaving school is legal in all 50 states.

Adventuring While Your Friends Sit in the Classroom is Neither Unfair nor Irresponsible

Doing all your college-preparatory schoolwork in six hours a week instead of the normal 40 (and spending the rest of your time adventuring) is not unfair, it's efficient. You're not cheating by cutting out the wasteful baggage that comes with school learning—classroom politics, disruptive social scenes, shuffling around hallways in 50-minute intervals—to instead focus on quality learning experiences. You're being smart.

Through the Macroscope

This book will teach you how to live life as an adventuring teen and still go to a top-choice college. If mixing adventure with college prep sounds to you like forcing oil and water together, I understand your skepticism. But it can be done. Paradoxically, I didn't find the key that unlocked both doors until I was in college myself.

My story goes like this: 12 years of diligent service in suburban public school graced me with a seat at UC Berkeley, the top Public Ivy in the US.[1] With high scores in math and the sciences, I entered under the astrophysics major—half inspired by the movie *Contact* (plot summary: Jodie Foster studies stars and discovers extraterrestrial intelligence) and half by the ego-stroking phrase "I study *astrophysics* at *Berkeley*."

That swagger took me as far as my third year, at which point I slammed into an intellectual wall: the first semester of quantum mechanics. Quantum taught me that astrophysics looks less like *Contact* and more like endless mathematical derivations—not what I had signed up for. If I really loved astrophysics, I would have sucked up quantum as a necessary speed bump. But I didn't. Instead, I began to see that my choice of studies was driven more by what school rewards (achievement in math and science) than by my inner longings. I plummeted headfirst toward an academic identity crisis.

As I sweated over calculus equations and entertained daydreams of dropping out to teach snowboarding, a friend from a one-unit elective course handed me a book written by former New York City public school teacher, John Taylor Gatto. This was the first line I read.

> I've noticed a fascinating phenomenon in my twenty-five years of teaching: that schools and schooling are increasingly irrelevant to the great enterprises of the planet. No one believes anymore that scientists are trained in science classes or politicians in civics classes or poets in English classes. The truth is that schools don't really teach anything except how to obey orders.[2]

Well, that was something different. Caught by a hook of curiosity, I put number-crunching astrophysics on the back burner for a few weeks and entertained a much deeper line of thought: questioning education from the ground up. Was it possible that my schooling—a training that implicitly promised the good life if one simply followed protocol—had merely taught me to follow protocol itself? Obeying orders had brought me to where I was now: majoring in a field that suddenly felt foreign and unsettling.

Gatto had my attention. I delved deeper. It's a small miracle what an hour on Google and Amazon.com can unearth. Under the surface of the educational mainstream I found brewing a deep and powerful countercultural undercurrent. Not every teen, it appeared, fell into the straightforward categories of high schooler or drug-addicted dropout. Some went to zero-curriculum free schools. Some attended Montessori or Waldorf or Independent Study Charter schools. Some were homeschoolers in the traditional sense of school at home. And some opted instead for the label unschooling: radically independent, self-directed homeschooling.

The unschoolers interested me most. These teens were taking on the college-level responsibility of self-motivated, self-structured learning at age 16 or younger. Beyond this accomplishment, however, unschoolers seemed intimately dialed into the most important of questions: what shall I do with my life? They appeared to take that question seriously at an age when most of their peers obsessed over clothing or video games. This question was where I was stuck. Could unschooled teens have something to teach me?

Years later I would sit knee-to-knee in a grassy field in Oregon with real-life unschoolers telling me stories about their international exploits, business start-ups, musical tours and college plans, giving me proof beyond doubt that success is possible outside of traditional schooling. But at this moment I faced an uncertain decision: to stay with astrophysics (and society's stick-and-carrot path) or set course for this strange new land of alternative education. Down the first path I saw a life of dutiful scientific research—but a life not fully my own. Down the second path I saw no certain end, only a bright shining light.

I took the plunge. I quit astrophysics and decided to take up Gatto's line of research: investigating the philosophy, psychology, politics and history behind modern schooling. Understandably, Berkeley didn't have a department called "Education History, Psychology, Philosophy, etc.," so I explored the options for designing my own major. Gatekeepers in Interdepartmental Studies argued that I couldn't switch from a hard science to a liberal arts focus this late in the game. I kept pushing, and eventually a sympathetic advisor pointed me toward a nondescript office in a quiet hallway where I found the woman who controlled the Independent Major, Berkeley's hidden design-your-own-major program. I proposed my new major (combining astrophysics and self-designed education studies), asked two professors to sponsor me and within weeks was approved by the university, giving me free rein to pursue my new line of inquiry.

During the next two years I feasted daily on an intellectual smorgasbord, taking both traditional courses and self-paced independent study courses, volunteering at a local free school, writing an honors thesis, traveling cross-country to interview authors, visiting school start-ups and designing and leading my own course on education theory (called Never Taught to Learn) that other Berkeley students enrolled in for elective credit.

Curiously, as my self-directed workload snowballed, I became freer. In my quantum mechanics phase, I spent 20 hours each week on endless mathematical derivations. Those hours *felt* like work. During my independent major, however, I worked more than 50 hours each week on homework and research, but few of those hours felt like work in quantum physics sense. My new major did not reduce my weekly workload (quite the opposite), but *transformed* it from 20 hours of undesirable *school* work to 50 hours of self-motivating *interest* work. In other words, I discovered that I became incredibly productive when driven by curiosity and self-designed studies. The emotional high from this epiphany rocked me at the core.

I graduated from Berkeley with honors (and a thorough disenchantment with my previous idea of becoming a high school science teacher) and set off on a nomadic career of outdoor education, freelance website design, working summers at a wilderness leadership camp and extensive backpacking. But throughout my work and travels, my thoughts always returned to unschooling and unschoolers. Who were these mysterious adventurers who self-designed their curricula, as I did in college, at ages 13–17? And specifically, how did these unschoolers get into college? College for me was an enlightening and exciting four years; in addition to finding myself through my conversion to alternative education theory from astrophysics, I relished the serious intellectual atmosphere and bustling social life that high school failed to provide. Was it possible, I asked, to combine the best of both worlds: an exciting unschooled teenage life and a meaningful college career? That question was the seed that flowered into this book.

In my research I discovered that two audiences were interested in the college-without-high-school thesis: teens who were currently unschooling and needed advice on how to meet college preparatory standards and frustrated high schoolers who wanted an escape path from school without giving up the option of going to a competitive college. I chose to write for the second (and larger) audience, under the assumption that current unschoolers could easily sift through my discussion of unschooling basics to find the specific tools they need.

After interviewing dozens of college-admitted unschooled teens from across the spectrum—from the Ivy Leagues to state research universities to tiny private schools—I'm happy to report that high school is not mandatory for higher education. You can live a life of teenage adventure and still go to a great college. This book will show you how.

Launch Sequence

Leaving school to pursue a self-designed, adventure-filled college preparatory life is both an exciting and terrifying prospect. With the tools in this book, you will chip away piece by piece at the terrifying part until you feel confident that you can live life without high school and not mortgage your future in the process. Here's the launch sequence we'll take to put this dream into orbit.

In *Chapter 1*, you'll radically redefine your purpose as a teen. Raised from a young age with constant schooling, most teens see high school as the singular purpose of their young lives. I'll humbly propose that *adventure*—intense learning experiences designed around your goals and dreams—is a truer purpose. And if you don't know what those goals and dreams are yet, I'll help you discover them.

In *Chapter 2*, you'll learn the basics of how to get into college without high school. Colleges don't care *how* you prepare to handle their workload as long as you *do* prepare. In other words, you can redefine the rules of the college prep game. I'll explain the five college preparatory results—intellectual passion, logical reasoning, background knowledge, leadership and structured academics—and the many ways to prove them on your own schedule.

In *Chapter 3*, you'll dissect your biggest goals (defined in Chapter 1) and examine each piece for its college preparatory potential. By combining college prep with natural passions, your hours of *school* work will shrink and *interest* work will grow dramatically. Throw in a few time management principles typically reserved for CEOs, and you'll be able to pursue your dreams, prep for college and have free time left over.

In *Chapter 4*, you'll explore the world of adventures made possible for the liberated teen. From international volunteering to self-designed internships to crashing university courses, a world of non-traditional learning awaits you. You'll hear stories from unschoolers who have had these adventures themselves.

In *Chapter 5*, you'll receive the final few tools that will make your journey a success. Conquering the fear of leaving school, the social life question and the logistics of college applications are all on the flight plan.

If you picked this book up and you're already in college, check out my guide to uncolleging in the Appendix. Here you'll learn how to apply the principles of unschooling to the college realm.

A Note for Parents

Prior to publishing, I sent the manuscript of this book to a half-dozen authors, researchers, students and leaders in the world of unschooling and self-directed education. Kenneth Danford, a former public school teacher and co-founder of *North Star: Self-Directed Learning for Teens* in Hadley, Massachusetts, wrote back: "You don't describe the role of parents very much. In your stories they seem to be not needed or mostly irrelevant. The implication is that they should mostly stay out of the way."

Because my careers have always involved working directly with teens, I was at a loss of words in my first draft to address parents on the topic of their child's unschooling. Ken reminded me that parents are an integral part of any and every education. Though I myself did not unschool as a teen, my parents were incredibly supportive of me and encouraged me to go on many adventures. The attitude that fueled my college turnaround was undoubtedly nourished by the seeds of self-reliance that they planted in my young mind.

What a budding unschooler needs from his or her parents is support. Specifically, they need your encouragement in their self-chosen projects, your guiding advice as they experiment with the world of work and your commitment to letting them make—and learn from—their own mistakes. This is the kind of support that Sir Richard Branson received from his mother when she stopped her car and asked him, at age four, whether he could find his way home from a distance of many miles away—a route unknown to Branson. He said yes, and she let him out of the car.[1] Branson later left high school, started his first business at age 16 and is now the billionaire owner of the Virgin brand of companies.

You are not irrelevant in the life of your unschooler. This book is packed full of adventures that your teen cannot accomplish without your mental, emotional and financial support. I wrote this book directly for teens, with little mention of parents, because addressing teens as fully responsible adults is the best way to nurture them into responsible adulthood. But I also did it in the tacit assumption that you are there in the background, providing the loving support that makes unschooling possible.

I wish you the best of luck in your family journey.

Redefining Teen

The Point Of Life Is Not School, It Is Adventure.

Let's begin this book with a bold proposition: You're in high school, and it bores you to tears.

Maybe you're frustrated by poor teaching or a melodramatic social scene. Maybe your eyes glaze over every time that you're treated like a child (or worse, like cattle). Or maybe your teachers are fantastic, your school brims with extracurricular activities, but you nevertheless sense that the world is much bigger than high school—and you don't want to spend another year in the holding chamber.

Let's propose that one way or another, high school doesn't challenge you. And thus, you're bored.

Unlike other people, I'm not going to suggest tips for perking up, trying harder or accepting the reality of high school. I assume you've heard the argument that you simply need to change your attitude toward school. Mine is a different approach. If you're genuinely bored, frustrated or disappointed by school, then I have only one suggestion: ***Stop wasting your time***. Life is made of nothing more than time, and if you are bored, then you are wasting your time—and not really living.

What is the alternative to high school tedium? My answer is: adventure.

An adventure, specifically defined, is any challenge that requires a lot of learning in a small amount of time. Traveling cross-country to teach rock climbing at a summer camp is an adventure. Crafting an online marketing plan for your friend's small business is an adventure. Spending three months on an organic farm in Italy to learn permaculture and the Italian language is an adventure. Walking into a physics professor's office to get book recommendations, working nights as a veterinary assistant and volunteering at a disaster relief site are all adventures. And going to college, too, is an adventure.

Because the word adventure drums up many more images than what I've just described, let me also tell you what adventure is *not*. An adventure is not an escape—i.e., an excuse to give up something that you've chosen to start but not yet finished. Adventure doesn't mean throwing yourself headlong into danger. And an adventure is not necessarily a physical challenge (like climbing Mount Everest); adventures come in many flavors, including social (introducing yourself to a hero), mental (writing a book) and spiritual (attempting a ten-day silent meditation retreat).

An adventure pushes your comfort zone, demands courage and requires determination. It's centered around your interests, your dreams and your personality. And most importantly, it must be chosen by you—not your parents, not your teachers, but *you*. More on that part soon.

To cure the disease of high school boredom, you need adventure. But adventure cannot be boxed into after school activity slots or one-week winter breaks. Real adventures take time—the time currently taken by high school. The radical idea I'm proposing, in other words, is that you stop thinking of school as your full-time occupation. If school does not challenge you, then leave school and seek adventure.

Bored People Become Boring People

Leave school! Butterflies riot in your stomach. No matter how ready you are for the idea of leaving school, a little voice inside cries, Wait, don't jump yet! This is the voice of eight+ years of schoolroom conditioning. It's the same voice that says dropouts become welfare-dependent drug-addicts! And maybe school will be better next year. I don't want you to squash this cautionary voice (because jumping without looking is always a bad idea), but I do want you to consider what will happen if you let caution rule your life.

What you have to fear is this: If you let yourself be bored in high school, then you will let yourself be bored as an adult. What does a high schooler who slaves away at meaningless, disconnected problem sets every night become in later life? She becomes the adult who slaves away at a job she doesn't enjoy, for less pay than she deserves, for a one-week vacation through which she would prefer to sleep. She does not spend the time she'd like with her children. And despite being a kind, compassionate and well-intentioned person, because she chooses to take orders instead of think for herself, she does not create the life that she wants.

Boredom is *powerlessness*. If you let yourself become bored then you load the dice in the game of life against you.

I'm certainly not suggesting that all teens who work dutifully in high school meet the fate of an unhappy or disempowered adulthood. School works for some students (i.e., it challenges them in the adventure sense), and it doesn't work for others. Most big, normal public and private schools work poorly for most students. Hence the very real threat of letting school shape you in a negative way.

Listen to the cautionary voice in your head, but weigh it evenly against the fate of allowing boredom to rule your life.

Homeschooling and Unschooling

To legally leave school, you'll have to become a homeschooler in the eyes of your school district; this is your quickest and easiest ticket to freedom.[1] But first let's get our terms straight.

I *don't* advocate becoming a homeschooler in the common misconception of the word. I don't want you to stay home all day, follow the state-prescribed 10th grade curriculum and cut yourself off from the world because other people's opinions are scary. This version of homeschooling, while it does exist, is practiced far less often than the media would have you believe. Homeschoolers are an eclectic group of educators with a wide range of learning and teaching styles. The flavor of homeschooling that best matches the adventuring lifestyle has its own name: unschooling.[2] Unschooling is a philosophy that places the responsibility for learning and growing in the student's hands. In this world, parents and teachers act as resources—not dictators.

Unschooling does not discredit formal learning (e.g. structured classes and curricula) as long as it is voluntarily chosen. Community college, four-year university, structured art class and a summer architecture intensive are examples of formal learning situations that an unschooler might openly embrace. High school-style classes—where students perceive themselves as captives and school personnel treat them as such—are not.

When not doing structured learning, unschoolers spend their time in self-directed learning. Emerie Snyder, a former teen unschooler and New York University graduate, poignantly explained self-directed learning in her college application essay.

> I consider myself an unschooler. The homeschooling community debates over what exactly the word means, but I define it as self-directed learner. My approach to learning is some-

> thing like diving into the pool of a particular interest, swimming around it a bit, following the current through a nearby network of streams, stopping off to explore connected pools, then continuing down whatever rivulets I find from there, and perhaps even ending up back in the lake where I began.
>
> By following one interest to another and recognizing their interconnected nature, I get a detailed and full picture of the whole network. The overall picture becomes clear as I explore each stream from within, and having a sense of the whole helps me appreciate the value and place of each detail.

Unschoolers take advantage of the best learning resources they can find to answer the questions that drive them. They tend to be independent, self-motivated and hardly ever bored. Not all unschoolers spend their time in around-the-world adventure like I suggest, but many do. Not all unschoolers choose to go to college, but many do as well. So while unschooler is an imperfect word for our purposes, it will do.

To lead a life of teenage adventure, become a homeschooler, legally, and an unschooler, mentally.

Unschoolers in History

If unschooling sounds appealing but still leaves you skeptical, I understand. In this book you'll learn that unschooling doesn't divorce you from the possibility of a normal life (specifically, in getting into college). But I'll also take a moment to explain why unschooling, a relatively unknown concept, is in fact a valid approach to education. Unschooling has existed and been practiced throughout the millennia, and by becoming an unschooler, you will join a long line of self-educating adventurers.

Maria Montessori

In the 1920s, Italian doctor Maria Montessori built the theory behind today's wildly popular Montessori preschools (and lesser-known elementary schools). She unfortunately died before publishing her full theory for the teenage years—what she called the adolescent plane of education. Montessori did, however, leave behind illuminating notes on her vision, from which you may ask yourself if the world-renowned Montessori was a closet advocate of teenage adventure unschooling.

Notes on the Goals of the Teenage Years

- Teens are newly social creatures. Unlike ages 6–12, where children desire to learn objective facts about the world (Why does this happen? How does this work?), teens crave discussion of moral and spiritual issues, the meaning of life and death and the exploration what others are thinking and feeling. Creative expression is their means for self-discovery.
- A teen's overriding interest is the dual exploration of the natural world and the world of human organization: commerce, trade and production. In nature they desire to test themselves, and in the world of commerce they wish to become helpful and financially independent.

Notes on Academic Study

- Intellectual study best arises from real-life discovery, both in nature and society.
- Academic subjects should interweave and heavily follow the student's individual interests.
- In a teen's life, adults are most effective when they act as resource centers and mentors in goal-setting (helping students avoid aimless activity).

- Seminar-style classes (discussion and debate) are more appropriate than lectures (which fit the data-gathering mode of ages 6–12).

Notes on the Teenage Years in Practice

- Teens learn best when living away from home, in communal housing, with both peers and adult mentors, from a few months to an entire year.
- Academic schedules should be flexible, with large blocks of uninterrupted time (typical of Montessori preschool and elementary). Teens should have significant practical duties, including cooking, cleaning, caring for animals, gardening and running their own businesses (like hotel service for visitors to the communal housing).[3]

In other words, Montessori advocated that teens experiment with living away from home, follow academic studies that match their interests, focus on discussion and independent study instead of lecture, do real world work, start their own businesses and explore nature while discussing life's deepest questions with friends and adult mentors. That's unschooling in a nutshell.

A Short A–Z of Notable Unschoolers

Unschoolers have existed ever since widespread compulsory schooling was invented. The following (very condensed) list of great achievers from the 20th, 19th or 18th centuries (or earlier) each left high school or never went there at all.

- Ansel Adams: Photographer of the American West
- William Blake: English poet
- Liz Claiborne: Fashion designer
- Samuel Clemens (Mark Twain): Writer

- Charles Dickens: English novelist
- Thomas Edison: American inventor (1,093 patents)
- Benjamin Franklin: Author, inventor and statesman
- Henry Ford: Industrialist and inventor
- Whoopi Goldberg: Actress, comedian and author
- William Lear: Inventor of the Lear Jet
- Abraham Lincoln: President and abolitionist
- Jack London: Author
- Liza Minnelli: Actor and singer
- Wolfgang Amadeus Mozart: Composer
- Florence Nightingale: Nurse, author and statistician
- Beatrix Potter: Botanist and author of Peter Rabbit
- Keith Richards: Rolling Stones guitarist and songwriter
- Frank Lloyd Wright: Architect
- Orville and Wilbur Wright: Flight pioneers[4]

Add ⅓ of the signers of the US Declaration of Independence, Articles of Confederation and Constitution to this list, and you'll get the idea that unschooling has been done before.

Churchill and Einstein

Finally, two of the most influential figures of the 20th century, Winston Churchill and Albert Einstein, credited much of their success to their independence and self-direction, two qualities not fostered by mainstream K-12 schooling.

> *Churchill:* "My teachers saw me at once backwards and precocious, reading books beyond my years and yet at the bottom of the Form. They were offended. They had large resources of compulsion at their disposal, but I was stubborn. Where my reason, imagination, or interest were not engaged, I would not or could not learn."[5]

> *Einstein:* "One had to cram all this stuff into one's mind for the examination, whether one liked it or not. This coercion had such a deterring effect that, after I had passed the final examination, I found the consideration of any scientific problems distasteful to me for an entire year."[6]

Despite its lack of publicity, unschooling is a time-tested and powerful educational philosophy. It has existed in perpetuity since the first compulsory schooling law was passed. Don't let the burden of explaining the term deter you from making the unschooling decision; all pioneers find themselves in strange territories with foreign names.

But First: What Do You Want?

After you begin your life of adventurous unschooling, what will you do with yourself?

A passion for freedom is an important element for success in unschooling, but it is not enough. Some would-be unschoolers jump out of school too fast, become overwhelmed by the sudden influx of free time and consequently give up self-directed learning and return to school. Don't do that. Smart unschoolers leave school because they've got better things to do—not simply to rebel. The rest of the chapter is dedicated to helping you discover what you'll do with your unleashed life.

Implanted Dreams

If I ask a group of typical high schoolers what big things they want to do with their lives, most will paint me vague images of becoming a doctor, solving world hunger or making enough money to retire young to a white sand beach with a tanned love interest.

Chances are that if you haven't spent lots of time grappling with your own dreams, you'll have similarly vague and clichéd goals. Of these goals, you must ask yourself: Is this really the apex of life? Where did these ideas come from?

Unless your parents gave you a non-traditional upbringing, your exposure to life has likely come through two lenses: school and the major media (television, movies and magazines). From these two sources you have absorbed a huge amount of information, much in the form of stories. And with these stories come messages—messages about what is important in life and how to live it. These are what I call implanted dreams. Some of them may be noble (like becoming a doctor or solving world hunger), some may be trite (like retiring young to a white sand beach), but each implanted dream is the same in that *it is not your own*.

Maybe your gifts are not in medicine; they're in journalism. Maybe ultimate frisbee makes you feel infinitely more alive than thinking about world hunger. And maybe your perfect date wouldn't happen on a white sand beach; it would happen in a mosh pit. Implanted dreams are dangerous because they, like most schools, are one-size-fits-all. And a one-size-fits-all shoe is an ugly thing that fits no one.

To some extent, every teen spends time trying on new faces toward the world. It's a part of growing up. But investing too heavily in the ideas of people paid to sell you things is dangerous. As with boredom, the teens who blindly follow implanted dreams become the adults who blindly seek the white sand beach vacation, only to discover that baking in the sun ten hours a day is incredibly boring. And even more damning is the realization that the white sand vacation doesn't make up for the other 51 weeks of the year that you spent working...for what? For someone else's dream.

The Dream Core: Excitement

My advice to you is to throw away every image of the good life given to you—unless given by a trusted friend or family member.

Real dreams are inspired by real life experience. Ask yourself what people really want behind implanted dreams: the silhouetted image of a mountain climber in a magazine, the tanned and fit bodies running through the ocean surf on a TV show, the hip dancers at a midnight club. Each connotes a feeling—the feeling of *excitement*. Climbing a mountain suggests the excitement of wilderness exploration. Tanned bodies running across a beach suggest the excitement of possessing physical stamina. Hip clubbers suggest the excitement of being part of an exclusive social group.

The feeling behind each of these moments is excitement, but I'll add one more element: What real dreams are made of is the excitement of *fighting against great odds*. Here's a quick thought experiment to illustrate the point.

The Iron Man Triathlon is an annual event in Hawaii in which racers endure a grueling back-to-back 2.4-mile ocean swim, 112-mile bike ride and 26.2-mile run. Competitors train for years to participate in an event of this caliber. Now imagine yourself suddenly implanted into the body of the Iron Man first place winner at the moment of victory. You would experience a quick emotional spike in reaction to the fame of winning, but then what? Your victory would be a hollow shell without the years of training and blood, sweat and tears that preceded the event. Because you did not fight for your goal (because it was hand-delivered and required no struggle against great odds), the excitement of winning the race would disappear.

Really living means seeking the excitement of fighting for a goal. Always winning your goal is not mandatory; most of us would be excited to simply finish a whole marathon. Fighting, and getting up when you are pushed down, is mandatory. So when you ask yourself, What are my big dreams and goals? the question you're really asking is, What excites me, and what would I fight for?

Finally, remember that excitement only comes from fighting for goals that *you* choose. Training for the Iron Man Triathlon is certainly exciting, unless your parents signed you up for it. Then it's one of the lower circles of hell.

The Question of College

Where does college fit into the excitement spectrum? I wrote this book for teens who want to both unschool and go to college — teens for whom the idea of four-year college is *exciting*. But does college actually excite you? Is college your own dream, or is it just another implanted dream?

Let's start by agreeing that college is not the universal ultimate goal of young adulthood. You can lead a wildly successful life with only your wits and determination, as demonstrated by the college dropout founders of Microsoft, Apple and Facebook (to mention only the computer industry). College diplomas are no guarantee of a fulfilling or financially independent life; observe the massive outsourcing of white-collar jobs. Four years of real-life working and learning holds the potential to benefit you more than four expensive years at a giant university. Learning to live a life of constant self-challenge is ultimately more important than any diploma.

Nevertheless, I wrote this book about college. I did this for two reasons.

Firstly, the college experience (college meaning both four-year colleges and universities) tends to be significantly better than the high school experience. What frustrated you in high school is much less likely to exist in college.

The biggest reason for this is that college comes in many different flavors, unlike the monolithic public/private high school. There are small liberal arts colleges and big research universities. There are sport-obsessed state colleges and academic-obsessed Ivy League colleges. There are low-residency colleges like Goddard, tiny colleges like Marlboro, independent study colleges, study abroad colleges and online colleges.[7] You have a much better chance of finding a college that fits your goals, personality and budget than you do a high school. And because college students are a self-selected crowd—unlike high schoolers forced together by age and geography—you're virtually guaranteed to meet people who share your values and interests.

Other areas where college excels in comparison to high school include: College gives you the space to pursue your individual goals; high school doesn't. College lets you set your own study schedule and attend classes only if you find them useful; high schools don't. And in college you're likely living away from home and taking care of yourself—an element of adventure that high school lacks.

Secondly, I wrote about college because even if college isn't for you right now, you can use it to your advantage. Precisely *because* our culture perceives college as the singular measure of success, doing college prep gives you *carte blanche* to leave high school and go adventuring. It's a bargaining chip. If skeptical adults argue that you're throwing away your future economic safety net by leaving school, explain that no future employer will care that you don't have a high school degree—as long as you have a college degree. With college prep in your pocket, you can go globetrotting, and one or two years later when you discover that one college that does indeed fit you, you'll be equipped to go there.

Because college is typically far superior to high school and college is a bargaining chip that will let you craft a teenage life of adventure, I chose to focus this book around college. And for these reasons I hope that you will *choose* college as one of your dreams—either as an adventurous goal in itself or as a tool that will help make your other dreams possible.

Dream Map Prep

The stage is set now to define your biggest dreams. But before you begin brainstorming, keep the following three guiding principles in mind.

Big Excitement Comes from Big Challenge

I recall a magazine contest from my days as a video game-addicted ten-year-old: the full-page ad displayed a big screen television, every video game system in production, full accessories and a dozen games cartridges, all of which you could win if you completed a series of increasingly difficult mail-in puzzles. My brother and I spent days working on those puzzles. We never won, but we still worked our butts off and had a good time. Why? Because the payoff was huge, the puzzles were nearly impossible and we loved video games. It all added up to a huge sense of excitement.

Most teens (and adults) tell themselves that their largest dreams are impossible to achieve, and they consequently set reasonable goals for themselves. The boy who wants to write a book settles for a more reasonable short story. The girl who wants to meet a human genome decoder settles for a chapter in a biology textbook. Being reasonable is hailed as common sense, but it's in fact self-sabotage in two ways.

Firstly, by setting a low challenge/low payoff goal, you immediately shrink the energy quota you'll apply toward the goal. Would my brother and I have spent hours playing detective to Super Mario and Zelda's personal lives if only a single Nintendo system was at stake? No way. If you're excited to learn how hybrid cars are built, shooting for a full-blown factory tour will inspire you more toward action than reading a few online articles. Baby steps are important, but only as steps toward something much bigger. Overambitious goals are the key to *seeding* any long-lasting ambition.

Secondly, with the whole world focused on reasonable goals, competition for big, unreasonable goals is surprisingly small. How many teens call the hybrid car factory and ask to tour the line? My guess is zero. Therefore, you have zero competition. You're not going to become an astronaut or make personal calls to Nobel Prize winners by simply wishing it. But if you're one of the few (or the first) in a field, and you've got a little perseverance, you can set the rules. Of course teens take personalized tours of car factories. Didn't you know?

Production is More Exciting than Consumption

Writing is more exciting than reading. Directing and editing a movie is more exciting than watching a movie. Coding a computer program creates a rush where simply using one does not. Production—the act of creation—is more exciting than simply consuming.

Consumption (of things like books, movies, computers) is indeed necessary to inform and inspire creation. But too much consumption leads to analysis paralysis: getting lost in excessive information absorption. Modern teens succumb far more often to over-consumption than over-production. Escape analysis paralysis by focusing dreams whenever possible on production.

Guilt is a Poor Motivator

Unschoolers tend to have a keen sense of social justice. This leads them to dreams of helping the homeless, feeding the hungry or saving the whales. Follow these dreams, but not at the expense of censoring your self-oriented goals. If the thought of performing Cirque de Soleil-level acrobatics (a totally self-oriented goal) makes you shudder with exhilaration, go for it. If you want to volunteer 80 hours a week for a nonprofit, that's fine too. But do it out of excitement, not guilt.

The Dream-Mapping Workshop

Now let's put it all together. To begin dream mapping, start with a blank sheet of paper. Turn it sideways. This is your map. You'll also want a few sheets of scratch paper for fleshing out wordings before putting them on your main map.

Dream maps begin in the middle, with your biggest dreams, and move progressively outward as you break your dreams down into smaller, more concrete steps.

Write small, because you're about to think big.[8]

Dream Mapping, Step 1: Define the Biggies

We'll begin by trolling for your biggest, deepest, most *unreasonable* dreams. Ask yourself the following two questions and use scratch paper to record every answer that pops into your head.

- What would you do if failure were impossible?
- What would make you most excited to wake up in the morning?

In defining the biggies, you'll notice that dreams come in three flavors: Things, Experiences and Characteristics.

- *Thing* dreams involve *owning* something (your own car, $5000 in a savings account or a new laptop).

Dream Map — Step 1

- *Experience* dreams involve *doing* something (traveling to India, meeting a favorite author or writing a novel).
- *Characteristic* dreams involve *being* something (a crocheting master, fully versed in Egyptian history or a world-class sailor).

Aim to create at least one goal in each flavor. To help spark your creativity, you can apply the first two questions to each flavor. For example: What experience would I pursue if I knew I couldn't fail? What characteristic would make me excited to wake up in the morning?

Write three to five big dreams in the center of your map. This example dream map begins with four dreams.

Dream Mapping, Step 2: Cerebral → VAK

Next, take each of your big dreams and scan them for *cerebrals*: abstract words and phrases that have many possible interpretations. Freedom and responsibility are quintessential cerebral words. Become an awesome guitarist is a cerebral phrase, as is save the planet, make money or travel the world. Cerebrals are not bad in themselves; big dreams often emerge in unspecific terms. Your dream to spend a month learning Kendo in Japan may begin as a vague desire to travel. On their own, however, cerebrals leave you helpless to take action.

If I dream to spend a lot of time in the outdoors (a cerebral phrase), I'll sit outside with my finger up my nose. If I dream to go on a long backpacking trip (less cerebral), then I can start researching trails. And better yet, if I dream to hike the 2,650-mile Pacific Crest Trail between April and September (not cerebral), I'll know exactly what to do. Cerebrals need modification to become accomplishable.

The antidote to cerebral dreams is visual, auditory and kinesthetic (VAK) language. Because humans ultimately trace the meaning of

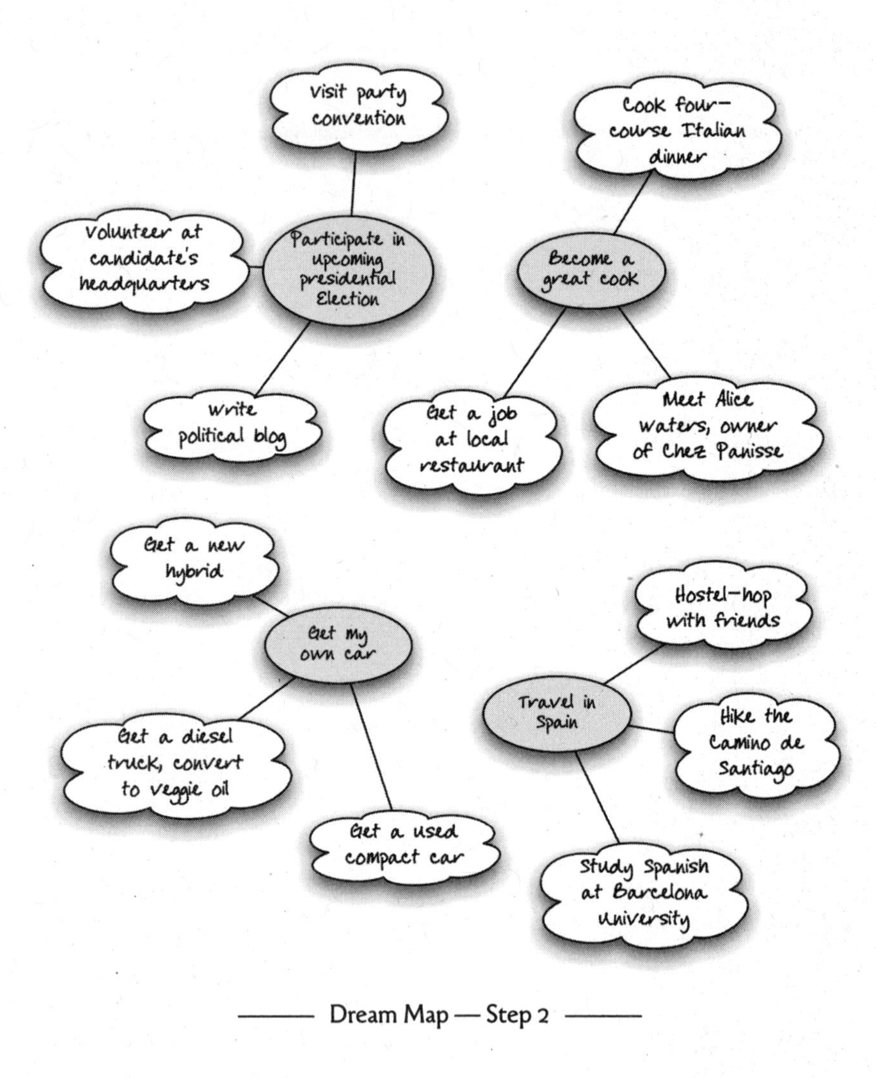

Dream Map — Step 2

cerebral phrases like "find myself" back to perceived (visual) sights, (auditory) sounds and (kinesthetic) feelings, VAK dreams have a higher chance of getting done. To change a dream from cerebral → VAK, write it in language that you can see, hear or feel.

Save the planet → Plant ten redwood trees in my city park (kinesthetic)
Travel internationally → See the Eiffel Tower, Arc de Triomphe and Parthenon (visual)
Spend time outdoors → Listen to the rainfall in a cloud forest (auditory)
Become an awesome guitarist → Play five songs on the electric guitar (kinesthetic)

Notice that dreams changed to VAK language become incredibly *specific*. They do this by including numbers (e.g. five songs, three places to see in Paris) and visual/auditory/kinesthetic details (redwood trees, rainfall). The more specific the dream, the more power you have to realize it.

Also notice that turning a characteristic dream (e.g., Become an awesome guitarist) into VAK language changes it to an experience dream (Play five songs on the electric guitar). This leaves you with only two types of dreams—experiences and things—each of which is straightforward to pursue.

Change each of your big, cerebral dreams to VAK language. But don't just do it once. ***For each big dream, brainstorm three VAK options. Draw them in bubbles radiating outward from the parent bubble.*** Three is a vital number because you'll later choose between these different paths to accomplish your dream.

Save the planet →
1. Plant ten redwood trees in my city park
2. Research peak oil and nuclear alternatives
3. Introduce five neighborhood kids to local flora and fauna

Become an awesome guitarist → 1. Play five songs on the electric guitar
2. Perform a cover song at the local coffeehouse
3. Read two books on music theory

Travel internationally → 1. See the Eiffel Tower, Arc de Triomphe and Parthenon
2. Visit relatives in Russia for one month
3. Build houses in Mexico over spring break

Spend time outdoors → 1. Listen to rainfall in a cloud forest
2. Run 40 miles each week for eight weeks
3. Learn to race dogs in Alaska

Dream Mapping, Step 3: Fat-Cutting

Now it's time to prioritize. Of all the VAK options you've just created, ***choose the five that really excite you***. If a malicious genie suddenly placed a death sentence upon you, these are the things that you would do before you died. You don't necessarily need to choose one option from each big dream. Just choose five and put a star next to each one.

Dream Mapping, Step 4: Baby Steps

With your dream map now narrowed to five high priority and accomplishable steps, it's finally time to get reasonable. Let's break down each starred bubble into three baby steps that you can start *today*.

Dream Map — Step 3

For each starred bubble, draw one more radiating bubble. In the bubble, repeat the process of brainstorming three VAK options. These are your baby steps. Baby steps should be totally concrete. They should be so concrete that if you gave a list of baby steps to a stranger, he would know exactly what to do with them. And unlike our previous VAK options, baby steps have a timeline.

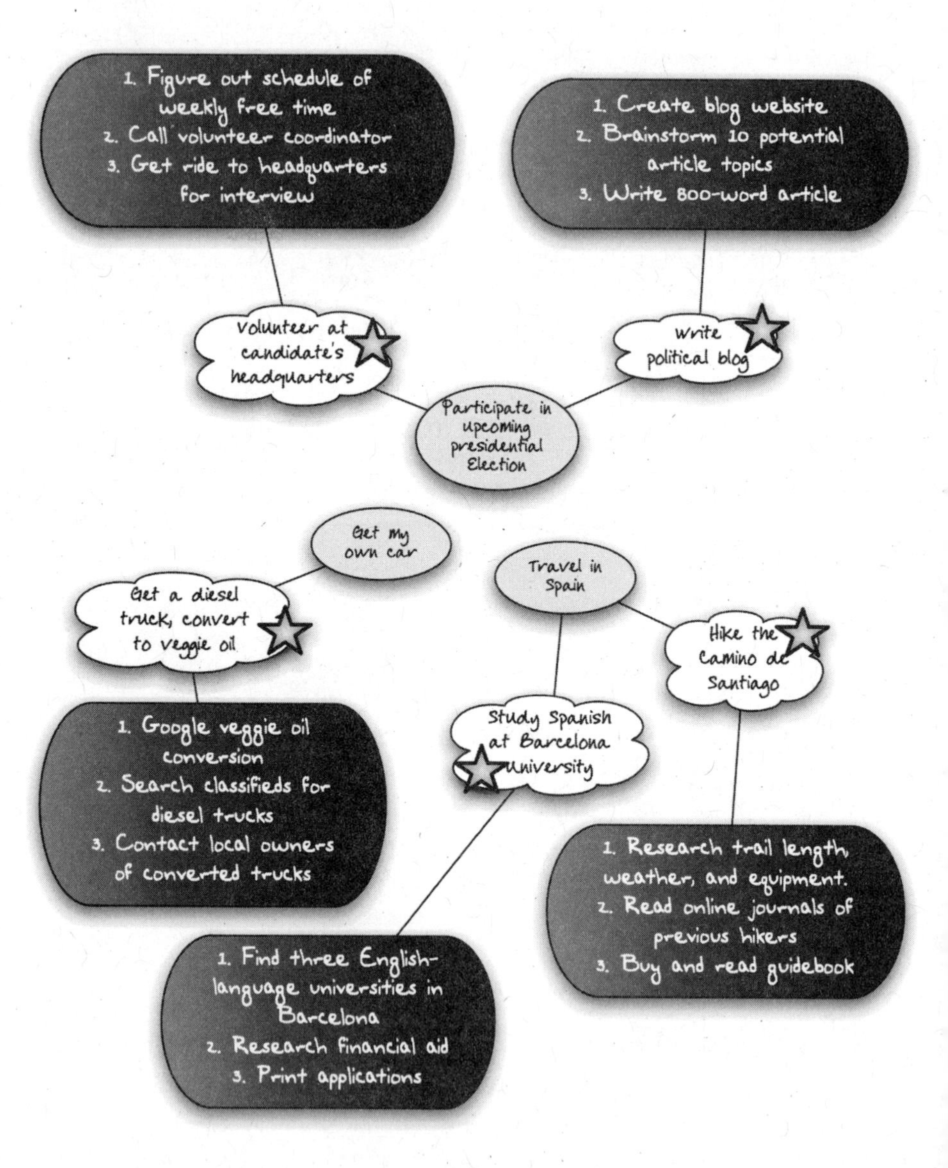

Dream Map — Step 4

Of the three steps you create

- **The first step** you'll take immediately, after finishing this chapter. It should take less than five minutes in total to complete.
- **The second step** you'll take tomorrow, before 11:00 PM. It should take less than 15 minutes.
- **The third step** you'll take within one week. It will rest on the shoulders of the first two baby steps.

Baby steps are the most important part of dream mapping. Thinking of big cerebrals is a relatively easy process, but only through concrete action will you discover which dreams are actually yours and which are implanted.

Your Finished Dream Map

Congratulations! A finished dream map is a beautiful thing—a practical and personal work of art. Keep it in a convenient location, like a desk drawer or taped to the wall above your computer. We'll call on it at various points throughout the book.

Create a Dream Book

The last step in defining your dreams is starting a dream book.

Dream mapping is a cyclical energy generator. After seeing the success of your first baby steps, your mind will flood with more and more dreams. They'll come at odd hours: in the shower, during a run or while you're sleeping. Letting a dream nugget slip away can be a sad loss, because if and when you remember it (days or weeks later), a chance opportunity may have passed. To prevent runaway dreams, use a dream book.

A dream book is a blank journal or notebook that you keep close to your body (e.g. in a pocket, backpack or handbag) at all times of day. Armed with a few reliable pens, use the book to jot down every dream, goal, VAK option or baby step that pops into your mind. Draw dream maps when the inspiration hits you. If you're a visual artist, draw your dreams in pictures. If you prefer, keep two books: one for spontaneous notes and the other for precision-crafted maps.

Jim Wiltens, summer camp director extraordinaire and mentor to my young adulthood, started his first dream book at age 14. His current book is over 30 years old. Jim (a more traditional adventurer) credits his dream book with inspiring him to

- maroon himself on a deserted island in British Columbia for an entire month.
- kayak on the Amazon river through headhunter territory.
- train and ride camels through India and Nepal.
- run the only roadless lodge-based wilderness summer camp in California.
- write six books (both fiction and non-fiction).

Jim's own hero for goal setting was John Goddard who, in 1940 at the age of 15, sat at his kitchen table and wrote a list of 127 goals, 109 of which he has completed today. John's teenage goals included such ambitious plans as pilot the world's fastest aircraft, read the entire Encyclopedia Britannica, study primitive cultures of the Sudan and publish an article in National Geographic—adventures that he immediately embarked upon at an age when most teens consider school the only point of their lives.[9]

Where will your dream book take you?

College Prep Without School

Results Over Volume

First, a thought experiment. Two students compete for the same seat at a top university's engineering department. The first student—let's call him Elmo—comes from a large, well-funded public school. Elmo's application assets include

- 3.8 High School GPA (of a capped 4.0)
- A traditional college preparatory course load, heavy in math and science, with two Honors and two Advanced Placement (AP) courses
- AP scores: 3 Physics, 4 Calculus
- SAT Reasoning Test score: 600 Reading/700 Mathematics/600 Writing
- SAT Subject Test scores: 650 Math Level 2
- 40 community service hours in a soup kitchen
- Letters of recommendation from Elmo's calculus teacher, physics teacher and guidance counselor
- A well-written personal essay on the soup kitchen, Elmo's vague interest in engineering and his favorite high school physics lecture.

The second student—call her Alma—left school in 9th grade to become a full-time unschooler. Alma's application package (more resembling an artist's portfolio) includes

- 3.8 Community College GPA (of a capped 4.0)
- Six community college courses (completed over two quarters): Calculus, Introductory Physics, Introductory Engineering, English Literature, Political History and Spanish
- A six-week summer seminar in math, science and engineering at the Massachusetts Institute of Technology
- Independent research on medieval war machines, including the construction of a functional trebuchet machine, documented with photos, schematics and journal entries
- SAT Reasoning Test score: 600 Reading/700 Mathematics/ 600 Writing
- SAT Subject Test scores: 650 Math Level 2, 600 Physics
- Six-month internship in a machine tool shop
- Three-month Costa Rica trip (surfing, volunteering and cultural immersion)
- Personal reading list including major works of fiction and non-fiction
- Letters of recommendation from summer seminar director, community college professor and machine tool shop supervisor
- A résumé showing items like a chronological history of studies, projects, internships and travel
- A well-written personal essay on decision to leave school to better learn engineering, the challenges of trebuchet construction and thoughts on the role of technology in developing countries like Costa Rica.

You're the college admissions officer. Which student—Elmo or Alma—would you choose for the engineering seat?

The Changing Face of College Admissions

You and I are not admissions officers, but we nevertheless sense that the unschooled applicant in our thought experiment, Alma, has a distinct advantage over cut-and-dried Elmo. Elmo did everything a college-bound teen was supposed to do, and he likely worked very hard. To him, working hard in high school was supposed to guarantee his college seat. But another student, without a day of high school to her name, might take it. What's going on here?

The rules of the college admissions game are changing. No high school = no college is an outdated myth. Let's look at a few of the new rules that make college without high school possible.

More Competition = More Opportunity to Stand Out

You don't have to be a media junkie to know that college admissions are becoming increasingly competitive. As high school guidance counselors watch dropping college admission rates, they tell their students to work harder. As grade inflation makes the once-coveted 4.0 GPA a more commonplace achievement, college-bound high schoolers resign themselves to even more hours of homework each night. A panic, however, is the best time to think smarter—not work harder.

When high schools chug out millions of college applicants, each chanting the same SAT, GPA, Community Service mantra, your opportunity to stand out by doing something unique with your teenage years multiplies. When admissions officers sift through thousands of nearly identical applications, the photo portfolio of your bike trip across South America and independent research on pollution in Buenos Aires shine like diamonds in the rough. More competition is an opportunity to stand out, not a reason to conform.

More Homeschoolers = More Non-Traditional Admissions Opportunities

The fastest growing educational movement in the United States is homeschooling. From 850,000 homeschoolers in 1999 to 1.1 million in 2003[1] and roughly estimated at 2–3 million in 2008 (accounting for projected growth and unreported cases), homeschoolers are putting pressure on colleges to create admissions policies for students without traditional high school backgrounds.

Applying to college as a homeschooler is not the indomitable challenge that it was in the 1980s or earlier. Admissions officers no longer spit out their coffee at the sight of a homeschooling course transcript. Unschoolers still find themselves explaining the concept of self-directed learning more often than not, but on the whole, the rising tide of homeschoolers has softened the path to college admissions for the non-traditional student.

You Can Flaunt Your Academic Muscles Without High School Classes

The four keys to opening the college admissions door, according to Ivy League admissions consultant Don Dunbar, are character (including maturity, social conscience and intellectual passion), a special talent or accomplishment, good standardized test scores and a strong school record (GPA and course choice).[2] Dunbar's audience is Ivy-bound prep school students, but his keys are nonetheless applicable to college-bound unschoolers. Pursuing your biggest dreams as an unschooler virtually ensures Dunbar's special talent and character keys. These two flowers grow slowly in the stale air of a classroom but flourish rapidly in the freshness of adventure and independent choice.

Standardized tests (the SATs and ACT) don't require school; most high schoolers study for these independently outside of the classroom. Advanced Placement (AP) tests are typically tethered to high school courses, but unschoolers can take them online or study independently and test through the high school. And other tests like the lesser-known College-Level Examination Program (CLEP), which proves college-level competency in various academic fields, are equally available to non-traditional students.

Three keys down, one to go. To obtain a school record, unschoolers have two strong tools: community college (also known as junior college) and homeschool transcripts. Community college is the quickest way to get a GPA and structured academic record that put admission officers at ease. Homeschool transcripts involve labeling parts of your unschooling projects with traditional subject names (e.g. physical science, art, sociology, math) and time quantities. When crafted with care and integrity, these transcripts give colleges the numbers they need to compare your school record to those of other applicants.

The Internet Levels the Intellectual Playing Field

The information technology revolution of the 80s and 90s (and continuing today) changed how humans seek and access information. In an earlier era, going to a central depository of information (like a high school or a library) may have been the best way to gather esoteric facts, but today, you can do that from your computer.

If you want to learn political science, you can watch university lectures via webcast. You can research the Cuban Missile Crisis on Wikipedia. You can read blogs by top economists, watch international protests on YouTube and get book recommendations from online focus groups. In light of these nearly free resources available at your fingertips, doesn't relying on a school library and an overburdened teacher for learning political science seem a bit outdated? The idea that learning only happens in school is a terrible crutch for any student who embraces it fully.

Some Who Have Done It

Don't just take my word that unschooling can lead to admissions to top colleges. Now let's listen to the stories of a handful of real teens who walked the unschool-to-college path in recent years. Of the dozens of non-traditional students who have shared their college entrance stories with me, I chose seven who represent a wide variety of personal interests, admissions strategies and academic ambition. What these students have in common, of course, is that they all have little (or zero) traditional high school to their names. The numbers in parentheses indicate their year of admission.

Charlotte Wagoner – Rockhurst University (2007)

Charlotte started unschooling at the beginning of high school, supported by her parents who had recently attended a speech by John Gatto about empowering young teens. At age 15 she enrolled at Penn Valley, part of the Metropolitan Community Colleges in Kansas City, where she took general education courses. After researching various majors and transfer programs, Charlotte decided that she wanted to complete her bachelor's degree at Rockhurst University (a private university in Kansas City).

Applying to Rockhurst proved quick and easy; Charlotte signed up for Transfer Day at Rockhurst and talked with an admissions advisor who gave her an idea of entrance requirements. The ACT and SAT tests worried her because she hadn't prepared for them, but Rockhurst ultimately did not require them of her. Charlotte applied online and was accepted with over 50 transfer credit hours from Penn Valley and numerous scholarships, declaring her major in International Business and soon enrolling in the university's 5-year MBA program.

Shannon Lee Clair – Princeton University (2005)[3]

A life-long homeschooler in the Los Angeles area, Shannon began studying lab science, history, English and French at Santa Monica

Community College at age 14. At 15, she took art classes through the University of Southern California's Ryman Arts program (a college-level program for high schoolers) that spurred her interest in visual arts, and she later won a stamp design contest that took her to Manitoba, Canada, for a weeklong arts fellowship.

Shannon regularly attended Shakespeare readings at her local library and produced plays with friends, including full-scale productions of The Magician's Nephew and A Midsummer Night's Dream. At age 17, she became an intern (among college graduates and professional actors) at the Will Geer Theatricum, which cemented her desire to go into theatre at the college level.

Shannon applied to many highly competitive colleges and ultimately enrolled at Princeton in 2005. Included in her application was a homemade transcript (with classes such as American Civil War History and Classical Thought and Literature), an official transcript from Santa Monica Community College, SAT Reasoning Test and SAT Subject Test (Writing, Literature and Math) scores and a list of her favorite books from the past few years. She also sent in an optional arts supplement that included pictures of her paintings and a CD of her recorded songs and monologues. Princeton did not accept transfer credits from the community college classes (because the school does not accept transfer students), but Shannon successfully tested out of the school's foreign language requirement using her French experience.

Andy Pearson – The University of Minnesota (2006)

Andy grew up in a Minnesota unschooling family and at age 16 enrolled in PSEO (Post Secondary Enrollment Options), a program that lets high schoolers take free college courses through the University of Minnesota. One of the admissions requirements for PSEO was a standardized test with reading, writing, math and science sections, and after browsing the sample test, Andy determined that he only needed to seriously review the math. The review took only three weeks. According to Andy: "I found that there was such a narrow range of problem types on the test that, if I learned how to solve a few basic types of problems, I could do most of the questions in the math portion of the test. I didn't regret not having studied math earlier."

Andy enrolled part-time at PSEO initially, taking one class per semester for two years while simultaneously dedicating much of his time to theatre. In 2005 he took the SAT, and with a recommendation from his PSEO Landscape Architecture professor, he applied and was accepted to the University of Minnesota as a full undergraduate (with Honors). Andy decided to defer his admission for a year to work for an environmental nonprofit, beginning full-time classes in the Fall of 2007.

Jenny Bowen – Wichita State (2006)

Leaving high school after the ninth grade to start unschooling, Jenny began pursuing her interest in ornithology by becoming an online authority in parrot forums where she researched and answered questions for parrot owners. She enlisted as a zoo volunteer with the responsibility of caring for 180 birds of 64 different species (which eventually transformed into a full-time paid position), and she interned for three years at an exotic animal veterinary clinic. When Jenny didn't have birds on the brain, she indulged her interests in nutrition, vegetarianism, natural building and homesteading skills, created artistic raw food meals with farmer's market produce, built an organic garden and became an avid bicycle commuter.

In 2006, with little more than a homemade unschooling transcript and ACT score, Jenny applied to and entered Wichita State University as a pre-veterinary biology major. The following year she took a semester off to live and study at a bird preserve in rural Mexico, where she hiked an hour each day to a cliff-side observation point to gather data on threatened maroon-fronted parrots and observe their interactions with the cliff's ravens, peregrine falcons, red tailed hawks, hummingbirds and white-throated swifts.

Siobhan Moore – Lesley University (2008)

Inspired by both her mother, an artist, and her father, a psychotherapist, Siobhan found her calling in the esoteric field of Art Therapy. An unschooler from a young age, she completed the equivalent of a typical, multi-subject high school course load in two years (at age 15) by working with a tutor (a local high school teacher!) and her parents. She then spent her entire junior year doing independent studio work and visiting art museums, at the end of which she applied to her top-choice school, Lesley University.

Siobhan supplemented the regular college application with a portfolio (documenting her art and music creations) and a home-brewed transcript of her studies. She didn't provide any letter grades or percentages for her various courses, but instead included written evaluations by her teachers, mentors and tutors—who also wrote her letters of reference. The one hard number that she did include was a modest SAT Reasoning Test score. Finally, two in-person interviews with Lesley admissions officers went very smoothly, which Siobhan credits to her extensive experience in talking and making relationships with adults as an unschooler. Lesley accepted Siobhan with early admission and additionally awarded her the $48,000 Edith Scholarship for the "interesting things" that she had done in her lifetime—all before age 17.

Emerie Snyder – New York University (2002)

Emerie credits her passion for acting to her discovery of the Wizard of Oz at age four. As a teen she enrolled in The Learning Community, a Maryland homeschool group, which provided her with a high school diploma and transcript for later college applications. Emerie took the SATs and applied to the prestigious acting schools at New

York University, Carnegie Mellon and Boston University, ultimately choosing to enroll at NYU's Tisch School of the Arts. She graduated in 2006.

Jason Crawford – Carnegie Mellon University (1998)

Jason attended a magnet high school in Maryland known for its math, science and computer focus, but he was ultimately bored and decided that he could learn more, faster and better on his own (having previously taught himself math and computer programming out of textbooks). After his sophomore year he decided to officially begin homeschooling. He focused primarily on reading math, science and philosophy books, took a physics course at his local University of Maryland and studied history under a friend of the family who had recently received his Ph.D. During the summers he interned with NASA at the Goddard Space Flight Center in the high-performance computing department, continuing the internship one day each week during the school year. In preparation for college he took the SAT Reasoning Test and an AP Computer Science test, scoring highly in each. He applied to Caltech and Carnegie Mellon University, gaining acceptance at both and ultimately graduating from Carnegie Mellon in 2001 with a BS in Computer Science. Jason later went on to work for Amazon and then a start-up company as a software engineer.

CP = *f*(Results)

What did each of these unschoolers do to get into college? They focused on *results* over *volume*.

Conventional wisdom says that college preparation (henceforth noted as CP) is a product of spending a certain number of hours in a high school classroom. This is the *volume* approach to college prep. Volume-oriented high school students assume that if they spend enough time in school (and ultimately graduate), they're guaranteed to go to college. And if they want to go to a better college, they spend more time in school in the form of homework, extracurriculars, advanced classes and community service.

In algebraic terms, let's phrase the volume approach this way: CP = f(volume). College prep (CP) is a function (f) of the volume of time spent in high school. The more time you pump into high school, the better your college preparation. Obviously the unschoolers above did not follow the volume approach. These students realized that too much high school was poisonous to them (for the reasons discussed in Chapter 1) and that there must be a better way.

There is a better way. Volume is a false standard. At the end of the preparation roller coaster, colleges want to see one thing: *results*. What is the result of a true college preparation? It is a young adult fully motivated, intellectually armed and voraciously hungry to do battle with humanity's biggest ideas in a community of equally motivated peers. If you can show colleges that you are this type of person then, no matter your methods, they will want you. The unschooler's approach to college prep follows a different equation: CP = f(results). College prep is a function of the results that colleges want to see.

What specifically are these results? Earlier we discussed four keys that top colleges want to see: character, special talent/accomplishment, standardized tests and school record. Removing these keys from the context of prep school, dissolving them into constituent parts and rearranging them yields five CP results that every college seeks.

1. **Intellectual passion:** a love of learning and a demonstrated depth of study in one or two intellectual areas
2. **Leadership:** a passion for taking initiative, both independently and within groups

3. **Logical reasoning:** the ability to identify patterns and make predictions based on cause and effect
4. **Structured learning:** the ability to work in a classroom setting and complete assignments under a deadline
5. **Background knowledge:** academic preparation for your intended field of study

These five results are what traditional college prep (high school classes, SATs and extracurriculars) are supposed to reflect. Every college preparatory trick employed by high schoolers, including community service, math camp, student government and class ranking, aims to prove one of the five CP results.

The unschoolers mentioned earlier used the magic of equation CP = f(results) to forget about slaving away in high school. They

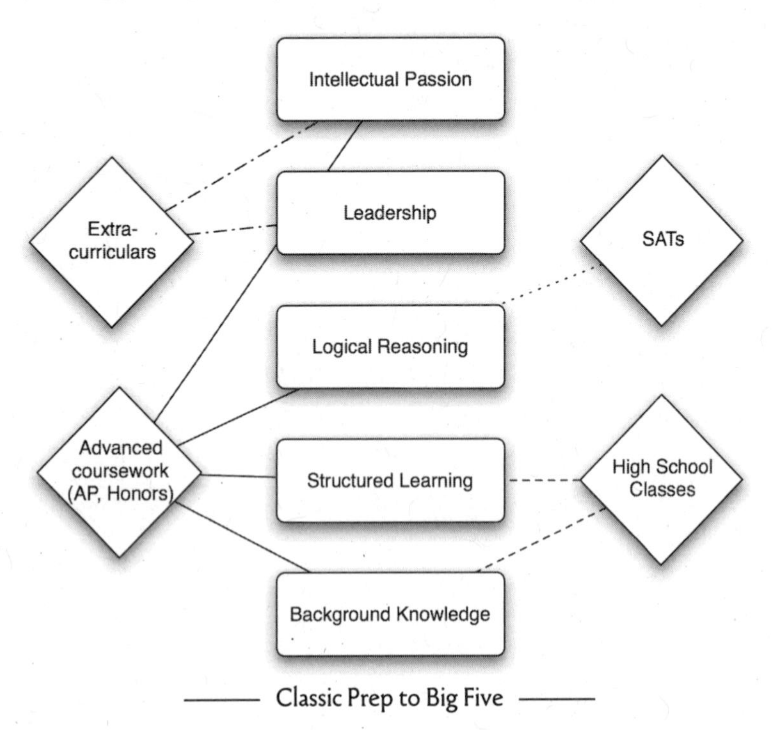

Classic Prep to Big Five

went straight to the source by focusing only on the five CP results. And you can, too.

Now we'll look at the multitude of options you have for proving each result. For each of the five CP results, we'll define the result, describe how Alma and Elmo employed (or didn't employ) it and suggest multiple options for proving the result in your own life.

The Best Buy Case

In 2003 Best Buy, the electronics store chain, was fed up with the inefficiency of their corporate office and decided to implement a radical solution: the Results-Only Work Environment (ROWE). While some other tech companies like Sun and IBM had offered employees part-time work-at-home schemes, Best Buy became the first tech company to fully remove the 9-to-5 leash, effectively telling their employees: Do what you wish; results are the only thing that counts.

Under ROWE policies, Best Buy headquarter employees started showing up for work at 2:00 PM, or leaving at 2:00 PM. They started napping in the office, bowling on Tuesday mornings, following Dave Matthews concerts across the country or retiring to backwoods cabins for weeks on end.

While common sense screamed disaster, the actual results of ROWE rocked the business world. By 2007, with 4000 headquarter employees on ROWE, the company reported a 35% boost in productivity and 50–90% decrease in voluntary separation (quitting). Workers reported that they were getting more sleep, spent more time with family and had more energy for work.

The Best Buy case put a serious dent in traditional corporate business thinking. By giving employees clear targets and the freedom to accomplish them as they saw fit, disaster didn't strike; everyone won.[4]

CP = f(results) is a ROWE for college prep. You're throwing away the blind hope that volume (sitting in a high school classroom) produces college preparation, and asking yourself

- how can I prove to someone that I'm intellectually passionate?
- how can I prove that I'm a leader?
- how can I prove my logical reasoning skills?
- how can I prove that I can handle structured learning?
- how can I prove background knowledge in my proposed area of study?

CP Result 1: Intellectual Passion

Constantly seeking answers to a driving question: this is the essence of intellectual passion. Rigorous question-asking leads to a depth of understanding and expertise. Prove that you've traced the roots of your questions as a hydrologist follows a river to its source, and you will prove intellectual passion.

Alma proved her intellectual passion through a multifaceted and in-depth pursuit of engineering: an internship in a machine tool shop, independent research on war machines, construction of a trebuchet and a summer seminar at MIT. Elmo's evidence of intellectual passion was a few advanced math and science courses. Because Alma blazed her own path in pursuing engineering, instead of merely signing up for classes placed in front of her, she more aptly proved her intellectual passion.

You can prove intellectual passion by

- **performing independent research**. The principle of research is simple. Ask a question, and then answer it. For example, Why is $E=mc^2$ such a famous equation? Start on Google, follow the scent and progress to higher quality sources of expertise, like the retired physics professor who lives across town. Record your progress from a state of ignorance to a state of understanding in a narrative essay.

Prove Intellectual Passion

- **internship, employment, volunteering.** When you intern, work or volunteer in your field of interest, you show genuine curiosity in the practical application of an idea. There's a big difference between someone who says I like biology because I took AP biology and I like biology because I tagged tree frogs in Costa Rica with a biologist for two months. Real world experience separates the truly intellectually passionate from the fakers.
- **in-depth reading and self-teaching.** Few high school students read out of interest. If you absorb a few books on your subject, you're ahead of 90% of the competition. After you've found the best books you can, take a top-notch college course for free online through UC Berkeley webcast, MIT's OpenCourseWare or Stanford podcast.

- **personal practice.** Interested in theater? Sew your own costumes. Fascinated by music? Build your own bass guitar. A chemistry fan? Disassemble a car battery. Programming your passion? Design anti-piracy software. Personal practice and production (beyond mere consumption) makes your intellectual passion obvious.
- **writing.** The fastest way to develop intellectual depth is to write. Writing forces you to coalesce thoughts into a coherent whole. Argumentative writing, in which you defend a point and respond to criticism, is especially valuable. Fumed about a politician? Write a short essay, submit it as a newspaper op-ed and participate in the ensuing comment battles. Verbal debate also works to develop intellectual depth, but writing is easier to document in the admissions process.
- **meeting experts in the field.** Get answers directly from those who've studied your questions for years. Track down an author. E-mail a small business founder. Walk into a graduate student's office. Get involved with the people who write the books, publish the papers and engineer the new designs.

CP Result 2: Leadership

Leadership is the art of taking initiative and making decisions, both for yourself and others. Each is important, but *true leaders first learn to lead themselves*. Build your confidence in making important decisions in your own life before making the leap into leading a group.

Alma proved her competency in making important decisions with a long list of self-initiated research and reading, international travel in Costa Rica, an internship and her community college record. Elmo's only non-school demonstration of leadership was his soup kitchen stint—a noble gesture, but also a conspicuous admissions gimmick.

Prove Leadership

You can prove leadership by:

- **Unschooling!** The very act of leaving school to chase bigger dreams proves that you're not afraid to make tough decisions for yourself. Most teens live a life of decisions made by parents and school. Becoming an unschooler to pursue a line of ever-increasing challenges proves initiative exquisitely.
- **Foreign travel.** International exploration requires constant personal decision making, and traveling with a group provides opportunities for group leadership. Note that I'm talking about largely *self-designed* foreign travel, not exorbitant vacation travel. Fill your travel with as many slightly-uncomfortable-but-exciting experiences as possible, like home stays or volunteer work, and you will build leadership qualities more quickly.

- **Taking leadership roles in groups and clubs.** Become a leader in after school groups (the ones that high schoolers join of their own volition). Become the electronics expert on the robotics team. Take scouts hiking.
- **Interning, volunteering or starting your own business.** The key to turning an internship or volunteer position into a leadership experience is responsibility: when other people depend on you to produce a real product or service, then you have responsibility. Starting your own business is a leadership no-brainer; you're running the show! If you have a partner or employees in your business, you'll find plenty of interpersonal leadership opportunities. And remember that employee can mean your older sister, a virtual assistant in India or a horde of neighborhood children.
- **Community activism.** Show initiative by spearheading a community issue that others are too busy or apathetic to approach. Recruit others in your cause. If you encounter trouble because a huge chunk of your community (school-aged kids and working adults) is occupied most of the day, try orienting your community-improving idea around the very young or very old (e.g. teaching computer skills to the elderly).
- **Self-initiated research.** Let's reemphasize the first leadership proof: unschooling in and of itself. Compared to teens for whom life=school, the sheer act of self-initiated research will prove your leadership qualities to admissions officers with great strength. Seek out the best books, movies, experts and websites to answer your personal intellectual questions.

CP Result 3: Logical Reasoning

Can you think coolly and analytically, instead of relying on impulse and emotion? Can you dissolve a poor argument into its premises and systematically refute each one? Can you focus long enough to

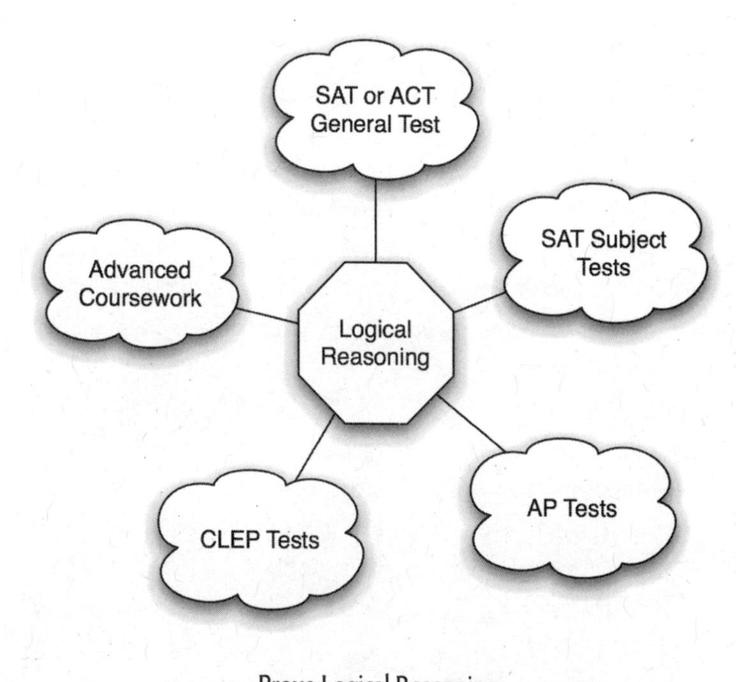

Prove Logical Reasoning

pull patterns out of raw data and predict future data based on those patterns? Any college worth your time wants to know that you won't crumple under a tough logic problem, and thus they ask to see evidence of your ability to reason.

For better or worse, most colleges rely on the SAT or ACT test to measure logical reasoning. You may not be able to get easily around the SAT/ACT[5], but the good news is that SAT prep is totally results-oriented.

Alma proved logical reasoning with the SAT Reasoning Test (formerly the SAT I), two SAT Subject Tests (formerly the SAT II), six community college courses and an advanced summer seminar. Elmo proved his reasoning through similar SAT tests, two AP tests and advanced high school coursework. In this arena, Alma and Elmo were equally matched.

You can prove your logical reasoning capacity by:

- **Taking the SAT Reasoning Test or ACT.** Which one you take depends on your target colleges. Start prepping early in your unschooling career for these tests; think of it as a marathon, not a sprint. Pick up two prep books (find last year's editions online for ultra-cheap), flip through, figure out your weak spots (as Andy Pearson did) and focus your studies accordingly. A myriad of preparation courses, tutors and strategy books are available for these exams.
- **Taking SAT Subject Tests.** These will be more important for proving background knowledge, but nevertheless, the Subject Tests demonstrate logical reasoning capabilities. Taking one or two of these (even if your college does not require them) is especially powerful icing on the logic cake. Like the SAT Reasoning Test, study guides abound to build your curriculum and attack knowledge gaps.
- **Taking AP and/or CLEP tests.** Advanced Placement and College-Level Examination Placement tests, like SAT tests, have study guides printed every year that make preparing straightforward. But unlike the SATs, these tests provide real, transferable college credits.[6] If you can summon the endurance to study and score highly on these tests, they will serve you as very strong tools in the admissions process.
- **Advanced coursework.** Colleges want to see college-level logical reasoning skills, so give it to them! Community college classes work incredibly well for this purpose. Enroll at age 16 (or younger), take a handful of courses, get As and Bs and you've proven college-level reasoning. Summer seminars (academically oriented sleep-away camps, often hosted by top universities) demonstrate equally strong advanced coursework. To find one, search online for your subject of interest plus the word camp.

CP Result 4: Structured Learning

This result is critical for unschoolers. Admissions officers wonder (rightly) if you, the intellectually passionate, self-leading, logically talented applicant will buckle under basic college structure. Will you consistently arrive at your 8:00 AM courses after years of self-scheduling? Will you exercise long-term planning to prepare for mid-term and final exams? For all the shortcomings of high school classes, they do accustom you to working on a schedule. Colleges therefore assume that non-schooled teens will suffer from procrastination and project abandonment syndrome. Prove them wrong.

Alma proved her ability for structured learning by taking two quarters of community college courses and attending a rigorous summer seminar. Elmo proved it by slogging through four years of traditional high school classes.

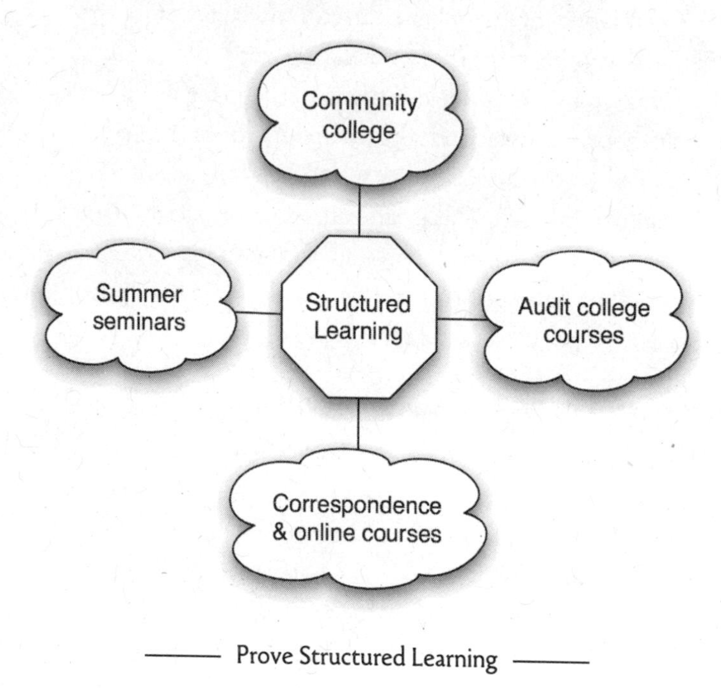

Prove Structured Learning

You can prove structured learning by:

- **Community college courses.** You only need a few to prove your point. Spreading the courses out among different disciplines—language, hard science, social sciences—helps to prove your structure-handling abilities in all areas of general education. If you have multiple years of high school courses under your belt already, that's great evidence, but still consider taking a few community college courses to show that school structure didn't overwhelm you; it just wasn't your flavor.
- **Auditing college courses.** Auditing means participating as a full student in a class at a four-year college, but receiving no credit. Freshmen-level lecture courses are the easiest to audit (more on how to do this in Chapter 5). Few teens ever choose to audit, and the benefits of doing so will be correspondingly high.
- **Correspondence or online courses.** A notch lower on the structured learning totem pole, but still decent proof, is a distance or online course with weekly assignments and big deadlines just like normal classes. Find copious options for structured distance courses with a quick Internet search using the above terms.
- **Summer seminars.** These hardcore academic programs wrap the equivalent of two or three advanced courses into a fun, camp-like summer structure. If you can handle an intense seminar, then you can handle a real college class.

CP Result 5: Background Knowledge

The final result you must prove is background knowledge in your intended area of focus. If you want to study organic chemistry, do you know the necessary basics of biology? If you're applying under a journalism major, do you grasp the fundamentals of grammar and syntax? Or if you're applying with an undecided major, have you given yourself a wide background in the various intellectual fields? These are the questions that college officers ask themselves about

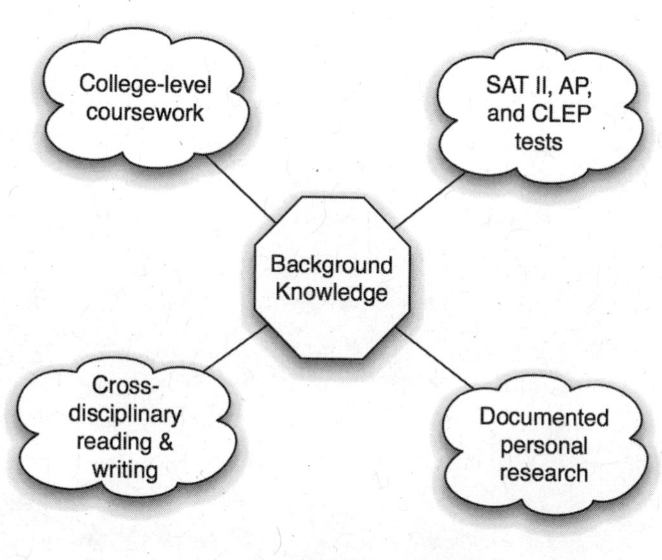

Prove Background Knowledge

applicants with self-designed curricula. Remember that most colleges ask you to take general education courses from across the academic spectrum. Even if you're 100% sure of your niche field, you'll need to prove your ability to handle almost any academic area.

Alma proved her engineering background knowledge by taking math and science classes, taking the SAT Subject Tests, attending the summer seminar and documenting her war machine research and trebuchet construction. Additionally, she proved general academic background knowledge with a diverse choice of community college classes in literature, history and Spanish and a varied reading list. Elmo proved his background knowledge through high school courses with a math and science emphasis.

You can prove background knowledge by:

- **Doing college-level coursework.** Community college courses and summer seminars work best, followed by online/correspondence courses and auditing. Any academic work that you can document (e.g. with a letter grade) can prove background knowledge.

- **Taking SAT Subject Tests, AP and CLEP tests.** Each of these test covers individual subject areas, thereby proving specific background knowledge. Each also lets you study at your own pace. Prove your college-level biology knowledge with the SAT Biology Subject Test, AP biology test or CLEP biology test. Support your intended creative writing major with the SAT Literature Subject Test, AP English Language test or CLEP English Composition test. Shop around to find your best-fit test.
- **Documented personal research.** Intent on studying political science? Take photographs and write five pages about your Hungary trip. Is graphic design your passion? Document your favorite graphic design techniques in a full-color instructional pamphlet for young artists.
- **Cross-disciplinary reading and writing.** Books are intimate conversations between an expert and you, frozen in time. Read them to gain breadth and depth of knowledge. Build an impressive reading list and then write on a few general themes to prove your integration of the books' lessons.

And a final note, applicable to all five results: Document, document, document! Track your progress with documentation. In the language of college admissions: if it's not on paper, it didn't happen. We'll discuss specific documentation strategies in Chapter 5.

Case Studies: MIT, Stanford and the University of California at Riverside

The five CP results are your ticket into college. But do your target colleges understand this? As a non-traditional member (unschooler) of a growing movement (homeschooling), you may have to hold the hands of admissions officers unfamiliar with your approach to learning. The best way to smooth their feathers is to tell them stories of other colleges—big, well-known colleges—who have already embraced the CP = f(results) equation.

To this end, let's look at three competitive colleges that have become pioneers in actively recruiting non-traditional students to their ranks: MIT, Stanford, and UC Riverside.[7] Use these case studies for two purposes: firstly, to use as discussion material when interviewing or negotiating with colleges unfamiliar with non-traditional applicants and secondly, as real-life examples of how colleges describe CP results in their own language.

The Massachusetts Institute of Technology (MIT)

According to MIT, homeschooling students have always been a successful addition to the university's community. Homeschoolers make up less than 1% of the applicant pool and student body, but the number is growing. The school has admitted students both with and without diplomas, and no formal diploma or GED is required. The factors that MIT considers for all students in admissions are "schooling choice, family situation, geographic location, resources, opportunities and challenges," and homeschoolers are not considered differently in this regard.

MIT suggests that homeschool students specifically focus on "[proving] initiative, showing an entrepreneurial spirit, [and] taking full advantage of opportunities" and they are most impressed by homeschoolers who "take advantage of their less constrained educational environment to take on exciting projects, go in depth in topics that excite them, [and] create new opportunities for themselves."

Most of the school's admitted homeschooled students used community college classes, online classes and other advanced courses that provide transcripts to prove many of their CP results. The school's free online webcast system, OpenCourseWare, is also a recommended learning resource. Many admitted students were active in extracurricular and community groups as teens, and a significant fraction took advantage of summer programs (examples of programs include CTY, TIP, PROMYS, MathCamp, RSI, Tanglewood and Interlochen).[8]

Stanford

Stanford's primary expectation for its homeschooled applicants is "a serious, rigorous course of study distributed across the humanities, sciences, math, social studies and languages." They ask applicants for a detailed homeschool curriculum/transcript, and they highlight that you need not "follow prescribed or approved home-schooling programs." They are more interested to read, in your words, the story about your decision to unschool, how you organized your learning and what choices you had to make to succeed in your unique path. And they recommend paying extra special attention to the SAT Reasoning Test (or ACT) and SAT Subject Tests in order to make up for a school record.

Stanford advises homeschoolers not to worry excessively about proving the social involvement typically demonstrated by school-organized extracurriculars. Homeschoolers, in their experience, demonstrate ample involvement in "community service, religious life, drama, sports, local politics or work."[9]

The University of California at Riverside

Our third and last case study, UC Riverside, differs from the previous two in its public affiliation. Public colleges tend to be more bound by inflexible admissions regulations than private schools and subsequently can be more difficult for homeschoolers to enter. But it can be done. The UC Riverside case study shows one example of how a big public university admits non-traditional students.

For homeschoolers, the school firstly requires a high school diploma, GED or a Certificate of Proficiency (e.g., a high school exit exam like the California High School Proficiency Examination). Next, they require either the SAT Reasoning Test or ACT. Lastly they ask for SAT Subject Tests in at least two different areas.

As a California public university, Riverside requires of all its traditional high school applicants courses in seven subject areas: history, English, math, science, foreign language, arts and electives. The school recognizes that you probably didn't take courses in all these areas, but nevertheless asks you to affix these seven labels to your various self-designed studies on the application.

Finally, UC Riverside asks all homeschoolers to submit a portfolio that "briefly summariz[es] key subjects the applicant has studied and learning methods used". They include specific guidelines with which to build your portfolio.[10]

Diplomas, Transcripts and Transfers

Finally, let's discuss a few subjects that always present questions for non-traditional college applicants: diplomas, transcripts and freshman vs. junior transfer options.

Diplomas

Private colleges, in general, don't demand high school diplomas for admission, while public colleges do. Our case study schools followed this rule. MIT and Stanford didn't ask for diplomas (or their equivalent), while UC Riverside did.

Getting around the public college diploma requirement is typically easy. Your basic options include enrolling in an online high school or drafting your own homeschool diploma with parents as signatories. These tactics work unless your college requires full accreditation. In this case, opt for the diploma alternative: the General Education Diploma (GED) or, if available in your state, a proficiency certificate from a high school exit exam. According to virtually every unschooler I've interviewed, these exams are much less challenging than other standardized tests. Be careful, of course, not to rely on any easy exam for proving CP results; just use them to jump regulatory hurdles.

Despite maddening bureaucracy, you can find exceptions to a public college's admission rules. Jenny Bowen entered Wichita State with no diploma because the school took her high ACT score as a definitive mark of college preparation; Jenny didn't agree with this reasoning, but she didn't argue with it either. If you're applying to a public college, talk to an admissions officer and try to make the college preparatory work you're already doing—SATs or community college classes, for example—serve double duty as diploma substitutes.

Transcripts

Our three case study schools each asked for a transcript, and expect that other colleges will too. Transcripts are the preferred medium for presenting your Structured Academics and Background Knowledge results. So how do you get one?

Transcripts are simply organized descriptions of coursework. You can make your own transcript (as each of the case study schools suggest for homeschoolers). We'll learn how to do this in Chapter 5.

Freshman vs. Junior Transfer

You have two choices in applying to college: as a freshman or a junior transfer student. Freshman applicants typically have very few or no transferable college credits gained from community college classes or AP/CLEP tests. Junior transfers typically have an Associate's degree (A.A.) gained by taking two full years of community college classes.

Community college, as we've seen, is an invaluable tool for the unschooler. Beyond proving multiple CP results, it gives you a taste of structured college classes, letting you test the waters before diving in headfirst. If you transfer with lots of credits you can have a four-year college experience less burdened by credit requirements. And in cost savings, community college is typically unbeatable. For these reasons, you should consider doing a junior transfer.

There are also good reasons *not* to spend two full years in community college. If you are fully desiring the all-encompassing, live-away college experience, community college will feel too slow and too close to home for you. Community colleges have much less of a sense of community than four-year institutions. And they are often filled with under-motivated high school graduates who reflect little of the intellectual passion that you'll find in four-year colleges.

Ultimately, the best way to make the freshman vs. junior transfer decision is to visit your local community college and a few target four-year colleges. Get a feeling for each and take classes, too, even if that means just sitting in on a single course. Then make your decision with evidence in hand.

Research Admissions Requirements at Your Target Colleges

We've covered the basics of the unschooler's college prep, but every college is unique, and different schools play by different rules. Use the following exercise to clear the fog and discover the specific requirements your prospective schools have for applicants like yourself.

First, choose three prospective colleges. If you haven't yet thought about specific colleges, start with a nearby state school, a nearby private school and a far-away trophy school.

Next, take these six steps.

1. Go online and search each school's website for the term homeschool (or home school). This may lead you immediately to the admissions policies for homeschooled and self-directed students. If not, continue to step 2.
2. Find the contact phone number for Undergraduate Admissions on the school's website. Because you'll likely hit a gatekeeper

when calling, also search the admissions site for the numbers of counselors, administrative assistants, vice presidents and anyone else who is not a robot who you might speak with on the phone.

3. Call each number and use the following conversation rubric.

Admissions: Hello, this is X University's admission department. How may I help you?
You: Hi, my name is ______ and I'm a homeschooling student from [Timbuktu]. I'm considering applying to your school for the [Fall/Spring/Winter] [quarter/semester] of [2022]. Can you please tell me if you have any special admissions requirements or advice for homeschooled students?

4. Follow up with an e-mail to the admissions department, thanking them for their help and asking any clarifying questions you might have.
5. Record your findings in the margins of this book.
6. Repeat steps 1–5 for every new prospective school. Getting ahead of a school's requirements is always to your advantage.

The Six-Hour School Week

Time Management for Unschoolers

We seem to have created a problem for ourselves. In Chapter 1, you outlined the big things you want to do with your life outside of school. In Chapter 2, you discovered the dozens of ways to do college prep without school. But both these activities take time. Where will you get the time to do college prep and go adventuring? Enter the world of interest learning.

My favorite illustration of interest learning comes from The Sudbury Valley School (SVS), a private school outside of Boston that enrolls roughly 200 students ages 5–18. SVS has no curriculum, tests or grades, and the adult staff members follow a strict policy of staying out of the student's way unless asked for help.

The story goes like this: a dozen boys and girls, ages 9–12, approached a SVS staff member. They wanted to learn basic math—the same stuff that kids are typically taught from grades 1–6. The staff member reluctantly agreed (thinking that someone had put them up to it) and organized a class that would meet twice a week, for a half hour, and leave with homework. He chose a thick, unadorned math primer from 1898 to work from, and told the students that they had to be on time, every time, or the class would be cancelled. They agreed and began working. Addition took two classes, and they quickly moved on to multiplication, fractions, decimals and percentages. Every student showed up on time, every time, and did their quizzes, oral exams and homework. And after 20 weeks—20 total classroom hours—each student knew the math cold. Six years of math in 20 hours.[1]

A zero-curriculum school that doesn't even teach reading strikes most people as a crackpot idea. But for more than 40 years, SVS has graduated young adults who go on to successful careers, personal lives and college (and typically their first-choice school).[2] SVS is not a school for the gifted; the school admits every student who desires to be there and can pay the modest tuition. The students who learned six years of math in 20 hours weren't supernatural—they were normal people motivated to learn by interest, not compulsion.

To create enough time in your life to do both college prep and big-time adventuring, we'll start with the same principle that motivates SVS students.

School Work vs. Interest Work

Simply defined, *school* work is work that you do not choose, and *interest* work is work that you do choose. Schoolwork is full of targets and goals irrelevant to your dream maps, while interest work intimately supports and furthers your dream maps.

Interest work is a straightforward idea, but it becomes deeply buried under years of traditional schooling and forced learning. Many teens think that choosing the subject of their English term paper is interest learning; it's not. Something you do out of true interest is something you would do regardless of how many gold stars or A+ grades were at stake.

Because arithmetic was on the dream maps of the SVS students, it became interest work. Most of the students, of course, likely didn't have written dream maps that included learn arithmetic as a goal. They *did* perhaps have dreams related to arithmetic, like build a tree house, learn about stars, feel confident that I am as knowledgeable as kids in regular school or even make new friends (the class being a social medium). But no matter their individual goals, the students shared the fact that they *chose* arithmetic, and they therefore learned it very quickly.

Full-time high schoolers are not incapable of interest learning, but their attitudes certainly become molded by too much schoolwork. This is why so many graduates leave high school totally unmotivated to learn *anything*. "High school is over, so I'm done learning" is their motto. These students have (falsely) decided that all learning is school learning, and therefore, no learning work is worth doing.

A stern teacher or parent might tell this student, You just need a more positive attitude toward school! This is like telling an Egyptian slave that he needs a more positive attitude toward pyramid-building. What you need is more interest work—and less schoolwork.

The Six-Hour School Week

If you're in high school as you read this, I guess that you do roughly 40 hours of schoolwork per week. This includes sitting in classes, doing homework, working on group projects and studying for tests. The amount of interest work you do in school depends on many factors, but I estimate that no more than six hours of your week is filled with school activities that you would genuinely do on your own. That's 40 schoolwork hours and six interest hours. Now we'll reverse those numbers.

To show you how this is done, let's return to our Alma and Elmo thought experiment. We'll analyze Alma's and Elmo's high school activities (listed in the beginning of Chapter 2) and see how much each spent on *school* work versus *interest* work in an average week.[3]

Elmo

Freshman Year

Elmo does traditional full-time high school—roughly nine hours daily (45 hours/week) of sitting in class, doing homework and working on projects. The work—disconnected from his life—is mostly schoolwork. Some class discussions and projects are exciting enough to be interest work—but typically no more than one hour per day (five hours/week).

Elmo's Hours

		Interest Hours	Schoolwork Hours
Freshman Year			
Fall	Classes	5	40
Winter	Classes	5	40
Spring	Classes	5	40
Summer	Summer Reading	10	5
Sophomore Year			
Fall	Classes (w/ Honors)	5	45
Winter	Classes (w/ Honors)	5	45
Spring	Classes (w/ Honors)	5	45
Summer	Summer Reading	10	15
Junior Year			
Fall	Classes (w/ AP + SAT)	5	55
Winter	Classes (w/ AP + SAT)	5	55
Spring	Classes (w/ AP)	5	50
Averages		6	40

Average weekly schoolwork: 40 hours
Average weekly interest work: 5 hours

Sophomore Year
Same as Freshman year, with Honors classes (+five schoolwork hours, +0 interest hours).
Average weekly schoolwork: 45 hours
Average weekly interest work: 5 hours

Junior Year
Same as Sophomore year, with AP classes and SAT prep (+five schoolwork hours, +0 interest hours).
Average weekly schoolwork: 50–55 hours
Average weekly interest work: 5 hours

Freshman and Sophomore Summers
Elmo does summer reading. Because he can choose between books and decide where and when to read, he gains more interest hours.
Average weekly schoolwork: 5 hours
Average weekly interest work: 10 hours

Total Averages
From the beginning of freshman to the end of junior year, Elmo averages 40 schoolwork hours/week and six interest hours/week.

Alma

Freshman Year (Including Summer)
Alma starts the fall with a full-time de-schooling vacation: three months of rediscovering interests, bike-riding under the sun, sketching dream maps and thinking lightly about college preparation. In the winter, spring and summer she does independent research on war machines, reads intensely and builds the trebuchet. Beyond reading a

few books that seem boring (but came highly recommended by family friends) and getting splinters while pounding nails on the trebuchet, all of Alma's work is interest work.

Average weekly schoolwork: 0–8 hours

Average weekly interest work: 40–60 hours

Sophomore Year (Including Summer)

Alma focuses the first half of her year on her internship. She also does more reading, and after discovering a few model authors, she's better at choosing books she enjoys. In the spring she begins com-

Alma's Hours

		Interest Hours	Schoolwork Hours
Freshman Year			
Fall	De-Schooling Vacation	40	0
Winter	Independent Research	40	8
Spring	Independent Research	40	8
Summer	Trebuchet Construction	60	2
Sophomore Year			
Fall	Internship & Reading	50	3
Winter	Internship & Reading	50	3
Spring	Community College	20	10
Summer	Engineering Seminar	40	12
Junior Year			
Fall	Community College	30	10
Winter	SAT Prep & Portfolio	40	5
Spring	Costa Rica	30	5
Averages		40	6

munity college and in the summer does the seminar at MIT, both of which are new, academically challenging and demanding of schoolwork.
Average weekly schoolwork: 3–12 hours
Average weekly interest work: 20–50 hours

Junior Year
Alma knocks out the rest of her community college classes, having learned a few tricks (like using office hours) to minimize schoolwork hours. She spends a winter of intense SAT prep and designing her admissions portfolio and then she takes off in the spring to Costa Rica to surf, volunteer and learn Spanish.
Average weekly schoolwork: 5–10 hours
Average weekly interest work: 30–40 hours

Total Averages
From the beginning of freshman to the end of junior year, Alma averages six schoolwork hours/week and 40 interest hours/week.

Our fictional character Alma employed the same tool that countless unschoolers do every day to craft a six-hour schoolweek: batching.

The Art of Batching

Batching is the process of combining steps from your dream maps with CP results. Added together, these two steps create a new, single batched step. A batched step then does double duty as an activity that both furthers your dreams *and* takes you closer to your top-choice college.

In our thought experiment, Elmo did not batch. He accepted schoolwork as his fate and worked hard, yet his years of toil produced a college application strikingly similar to thousands of other applicants. Alma, on the other hand, was a batching queen. She had fun, followed her dreams and did the necessary college prep at the same time. Her college application stood out of the crowd (actually, it jumped and screamed out of the crowd).

Alma was batching when she used community college to learn engineering *and* prove Structured Learning and Background Knowledge; when she interned at a machine shop to gain skills *and* prove Intellectual Passion and when she traveled to Costa Rica to learn surfing *and* prove Leadership.

Understand that batching is not about radically shifting your goals to make them more college-friendly. Don't give up your backyard permaculture experiment to read a biology textbook or replace your self-published magazine with a five-paragraph essay. Finding new and different way to express your interest-based activities in CP terms is always possible; regaining lost opportunities to pursue your dreams as a teen is not.

Basic batching is straightforward, and through our discussion you've already gathered the tools necessary to begin.

1. Examine your dream map.
2. Examine the descriptions of the five CP results (Chapter 2).
3. For each pair of steps that overlap, create a new, batched step.

This is basic batching. Academically related dreams (e.g. those involving engineering, poetry or political science) batch easily with CP steps. No additional thought experiments are necessary to illustrate basic batching.

But what about your dreams and goals that are not academically related? Adventurous unschoolers often find themselves daydreaming about epic bike rides, wandering around foreign countries, spending long hours in their garden and other non-academic activities. This is when batching gets more tricky. For these cases, let's look at an example of complex batching in action with a distinctly non-academic goal: a long-distance backpacking trip.

A Batching Example: Gia and the PCT

Gia's biggest dream is to hike the 2,650-mile Pacific Crest Trail (PCT), a five-month backpacking trip from the Mexican to Canadian borders through California, Oregon and Washington. The PCT absolutely dominates her dream map, but Gia also plans to apply to UC Santa Barbara, Pepperdine and a few other competitive colleges for a Marine Biology major. At age 16, she has another year and a half before she plans to go to college. How does Gia batch her PCT dream with the college prep she also wants to accomplish?

1. Gia starts by redrawing her dream map to focus only on the PCT. She crafts five big dreams that will make her trip possible.

- Obtain safety training
- Learn flora, fauna and geology of western states
- Gain map and compass skills
- Perform hike pre-training
- Research thru-hiking strategy (including food resupply, lightweight gear and advice from previous hikers)

She then brainstorms three VAK options for each big dream.

Safety Training

- Take a three-day Wilderness First Aid (WFA) course
- Take a ten-day Wilderness First Responder (WFR) course
- Take notes from a WFA book at a local bookstore

Western flora, fauna and geology

- Enroll in ecology and geology courses at community college
- Audit ecology and geology courses at local university
- Self-teach with library books, university webcasts and Internet research

Map and Compass

- Join an orienteering group and attend five weekend map and compass geocaching treasure hunts
- Library and online research
- Practice during one-night trip in local wilderness

Hike Pre-Training

- One-week trip on John Muir Trail
- Take biweekly day hikes in local hills, increasing distance from two miles to ten miles
- Join community track team

Thru-hiking Research

- Read three-part PCT guidebook series
- Read Yogi's Guide for PCT thru-hikers
- Contact and interview the author of the PCT documentary DVD, Walk

2. To begin batching, Gia scans her VAK options for potential CP overlap. She determines that she can

- prove *structured learning* through WFA/WFR courses, community college ecology and geology courses or auditing university ecology and geology courses.
- prove *leadership* by becoming an community organizer for the geocaching group, initiating contact with the DVD documentary author, leading a one-week trip on the John Muir Trail or becoming WFR certified.
- prove *logical reasoning* by doing for-credit coursework in either community college or auditing the university ecology and geology courses.
- prove *background knowledge* with any of the college-level courses or self-designed (and documented) library and Internet

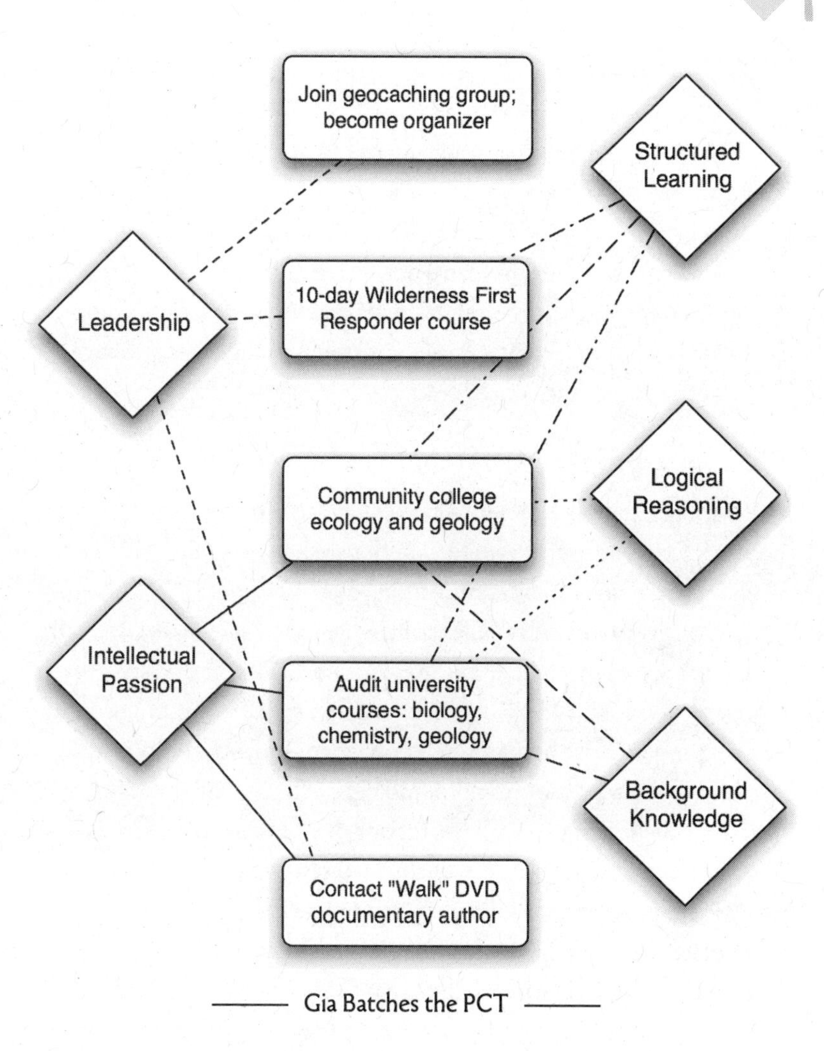

Gia Batches the PCT

research in biology, chemistry, geology and other prerequisite fields for marine biology.

- prove *intellectual passion* through any self-initiated research or meeting the Walk documentary author.

3. She identifies the five options with the most CP overlap.

- Joining the geocaching group as an organizer

- Taking the ten-day WFR safety training course
- Enrolling in the community college courses
- Auditing the university courses
- Interviewing the Walk documentary author

4. Finally, Gia makes these five options her priority and creates three concrete baby steps for each one. And *voilà*! She is on her way to both hiking the Pacific Crest Trail and going to college at the same time.

Conquering the Unbatchables

With batching under your belt, you'll be able to combine a significant fraction of your dream map options with CP results. This alone will turn you into an interest learning machine.

Not every important CP result, however, will connect to your dream map. For example, the SAT, AP and CLEP tests (which prove logical reasoning) virtually never batch well. Or the philosophy books required (as background knowledge) for your rhetoric major might seem impossibly mind-numbing. But all five CP results are vital for college admissions. If you let one or two results become weak, your entire college plan may become compromised.

Facing the *unbatchables*—college preparatory tasks completely unrelated to your other dreams—is unavoidable. This is why we have a six-hour schoolweek instead of a zero-hour schoolweek. But we won't dwell on these less savory challenges in the college admissions process; we'll conquer them with two time management principles from the world of business.

The Time Management Case Study: Learning Chemistry

Let's imagine that you've done all the prep work necessary to enter your top-choice college as an English major, with one glaring hole: a prerequisite class in chemistry. This part of the science background knowledge (required of all incoming freshmen) has proved itself unbatchable for you. Physics and biology were palatable, and sometimes even enjoyable; but chemistry left you lifeless, and you never took the initiative to get it done early. Now you just want to do the chemistry, prove your background knowledge and move on with life.

To conquer this piece of background knowledge, you scan over your CP options. Because the chemistry required is lab chemistry, you decide that reading and writing alone would not do the trick. A research project is an option. The SAT, AP and CLEP tests in chemistry are options. And taking a college-level course is also an option. But you want to get this done as quickly as possible, and a formal course via community college or a university might move too slowly. The research project option is also dodgy, in the sense that you'd have to do a really in-depth project to use it as an equivalent for a high school course. Your last options are the tests. Researching the three options online, you decide to use the CLEP chemistry test, which proves competency equal to a one-year general chemistry course.

The 90-minute, 75-question CLEP chemistry test is fully outlined on the College Board website. You know what you have to study. Some of the topics look familiar and others totally foreign. At this point, the first question to ask yourself becomes: How much time should I dedicate to studying for this exam?

Parkinson's Law

Defining the amount of time you'll spend on a project is the critical first step in unschooling time management. Common sense tells you to give yourself plenty of time to get an important task done. Forget common sense in this case. To tackle a big project, begin by giving yourself an *unreasonably small* time quota.

Practically speaking, you want to keep your schoolwork hours to a minimum. If you can learn chemistry in eight weeks at four hours per week instead of 30 weeks at eight hours per week (high school quantities), do it. But more importantly, a short deadline is superior to a long one because it has the psychological effect of making you do more work. This is Parkinson's Law.

In 1955, Cyril Northcote Parkinson, a British professor, cleverly observed in a satirical article that government bureaucracies tend to create meaningless work for themselves if given the opportunity. His theory became popularly known as Parkinson's Law: the principle that *work expands to fill the time available for its completion*. Applied to the realm of personal productivity, this means that the more time someone has to do work, the more he will imagine all sorts of new tasks (unrelated to the core goal) to fill that time.

To illustrate Parkinson's Law, imagine that you are an office intern. I am your intern supervisor. I assign you a mission-critical task: research all the Thai restaurants in the city and choose one to host a big company dinner. The dinner is in one week, and you have three days to complete your research.

Because this task apparently requires nothing more than an online search and a few phone calls, you see no reason for hasty action. You spend the first of your three days browsing restaurant websites and reading reviews. With success close at hand, you spend the second day researching the intricacies of Thai spices. And on the third day you finally call a restaurant and make a reservation, but not before browsing flight prices to Thailand because all this research has made you hungry for some authentic *pad thai*.

In the end, you successfully completed the task: making the dinner reservation. But you also spent hours doing unnecessary or excessive research. Because you are only an intern in this example, your wasted time falls on other's shoulders. But when you schedule your own time as an unschooler, wasted time is always *your* time. In our example, the naïve supervisor is at fault. I should have given you 30 minutes to perform the restaurant research—and get me a soy latte while you're at it. With only a half hour you would have condensed your actions into only those absolutely necessary for the task: finding restaurants, reading reviews and making the reservation.

Work expands to fill the time available for its completion. Give your schoolwork projects an unreasonably short deadline, and you set yourself up to focus only on essentials.

The 80/20 Rule

With a short deadline set, you now face the second big question: How do I choose my study materials?

You have an outline of the CLEP chemistry test (including practice tests for previous years), so you know which topics you need to hit. But the sheer volume of chemistry preparation options out there is huge. Which is the best for your purpose? Which will take you most quickly from non-competency to competency? Enter our second time management principle: the 80/20 Rule.

Italian economist Vilfredo Pareto noticed a unique phenomenon while studying peapods in his garden. Roughly 20% of the pods consistently produced 80% of the peas that he harvested. Strangely enough, he also found this pattern in the uneven distribution of wealth in industrial societies. In his approximation, 80% of the wealth in a society was created by roughly 20% of the producers. Putting peas and people together, the Pareto Principle thus emerged: *80% of outcomes flow from 20% of inputs*.

The Pareto Principle came into vogue in the business world as The 80/20 Rule, and it has use across multiple areas of life. Think back to the last time you typed a big essay for school. What percent of your computer time were you in focused writing mode, and what percent were you surfing the web, instant messaging, day dreaming or making irrelevant edits? Chances are that 20% of the time you physically spent at the computer produced 80% of the quality of your essay. 80% of your results flow from 20% of your efforts.

Here are two more examples. Of all your high school teachers, who connects with you and inspires you? My guess is one out of five teachers (20%). The others are just wallpaper. But that one great teacher makes up for the rest of them: 80% of the benefits flow from 20% of the inputs. Now do it in reverse: what 20% of the people in your life give you 80% of your trouble and hassle? Perhaps it's an irresponsible friend or a stupid high school clique. How much would your life improve if you removed those people from the equation? 80% of stress flows from 20% of stressors.

So how do you apply the 80/20 rule to learning chemistry? Start by figuring out what all (100%) of your options are for teaching yourself the subject. An Internet search and library visit reveals thick textbooks, quick reference pamphlets, university webcast lectures, CLEP-specific study guides and free test prep websites available at your fingertips. Let's also assume that have at least one friend who is a chemistry whiz. Those are your options.

Now ask yourself, of the 100% of available options for learning chemistry, which 20% will do the job the most quickly and effectively? Quick means that the materials are intelligible to you, and effective means that they're focused on specific topics that you need to pass the exam. Perhaps you find the webcast lectures illuminating (and the navigation controls let you zip quickly between specific topics). Browsing CLEP study guides in the bookstore, you find one guide in particular that speaks to you. The textbooks are too deep and the pamphlets too shallow; the free websites are too distracting and your friend is too busy. So you settle on the webcast and CLEP guide as your 20%.

Choosing materials wisely is the key function of the 80/20 principle. As you practice the principle, you will become better at finding the resources that work for you and removing those that don't. The other 80% of materials you shouldn't entirely discount, of course, because they might prove useful in the future.

80/20 and Parkinson's Law Combined

With your options for learning chemistry now narrowed down to two resources and a tight deadline set, you are ready to achieve maximum schoolwork efficiency.

In the schedule that you've set to prepare for the exam (i.e. eight weeks, four hrs/day), focus only on the resources that you have chosen: the university webcast and CLEP prep book. Because your deadline is short, you will be psychologically motivated to work hard, and because the resources you have chosen are the few (20%) that appeal most to you, you will learn quickly. And come testing time, you will have fulfilled your college's chemistry requirement faster than any of its other applicants.

Time Management Solved

How will you motivate yourself to do college prep without school? This is one of the top questions asked of unschoolers. Now you have the answer.

With interest learning and batching, unschoolers do college prep out of self-motivation. With Parkinson's Law and the 80/20 Rule, they condense unbatchable schoolwork into the six-hour schoolweek. And they still have time left over for adventure.

The Adventure Blender

Ideas for High-Impact Adventure

To appreciate the sheer vastness of America one could do many, many things.

One could read the accounts of William Clark and Meriwether Lewis as they mapped the western territories.

One could board an airplane and plaster their face to the window, watching cities turn to farmlands turn to mountains turn to long stretches of rocky, sandy coast.

One could spend months in a car with beatnik overtones, feeling the country in one's very body as ears pop in the mountains and wrists sweat in the south, watching gas prices change state to state.

Or one could simply look at a US map, keeping in mind that every fingernail is a mile or more.

However, if you're pressed for time, short on money, and don't feel like reading the adventures of Lewis and Clark, you could simply grab a friend by the shoulder and whisper conspiratorially in his ear, "hey, do you wanna ride bikes to

Baltimore this weekend?" and—I guarantee this—you will suddenly appreciate the enormity of our country.

I did.

I do.

—Dave Thomas, age 17 unschooler, rode 100 miles in 12 hours from Philadelphia to Baltimore.

Time to refocus on *adventure*. An adventure (as defined in Chapter 1) is any challenge that requires a lot of learning in a small amount of time. You brainstormed many potential adventures in the dream mapping workshop. Now let's add more fuel to the fire by introducing you to a few *optimal adventures*: some of the most exciting frameworks for packing lots of learning into a small period of time. These adventures, as always, will center around your interests and dreams. And now that you're versed in the language of CP results (Chapter 2), we'll note which results each adventure can prove.

Get your dream map out when reading the pages that follow. The following ideas will inspire you to modify or fully rewrite your map with bigger, grander and, well, more adventurous adventures.

Internships

Jenny Bowen's hand was trembling. Few people get to handle a live parrot, let alone tube-feed a sick parrot back to health. But at age 16, Jenny was doing just this as an intern at the Prairie Avian & Exotic Animal Clinic in Wichita, Kansas.

Beyond aiding the doctor with neutering rabbits, rat tumor removals, skunk de-scenting and shaving mice, Jenny held a number of other responsibilities during her three-year internship: assisting with examinations, tending to injured and orphaned wildlife, delivering microbiological samples to the local university, answering phone calls and running the store. When the office was slow she read and chatted up the colorful, often eccentric pet owners in the waiting room. In the second year of the internship, the doctor gave Jenny the keys to the building and started paying her a small stipend.

Becoming an avian veterinarian is Jenny's dream. Some of her other unschooling adventures nudged her toward becoming a vet, like volunteering as an endangered bird keeper at the county zoo, but she credits the internship as her largest influence. Jenny says: "Being able to dissect euthanized animals or just watching surgeries while having somebody to explain was better than any biology class I could have taken!"

Today, Jenny studies biology at Wichita State University in preparation for veterinary school. In her spare time she teaches and performs violin, grows vegetables and organizes ultimate frisbee games. She looks forward to her future career—a career ultimately inspired by an intern's opportunity to tube-feed parrots.

The word internship covers a wide variety of unpaid (or low-paid) work opportunities. Three big opportunities that you'll find under this umbrella include

1. highly advertised summer internships with large companies.
2. apprenticeships in the technical trades (e.g. carpentry).
3. unpublicized (and possibly not yet imagined) internships in small enterprises.

For the purposes of this book, we'll focus only on the third opportunity: unpublicized and informal internships with small enterprises. (Note that by the word enterprise we can mean a business, a nonprofit business or a non-business entity like a volunteer organization.)

We won't bother with summer internships at big companies because there's simply too much competition for not enough opportunity. You'll be competing with *volume*-oriented coat-and-tie high schoolers gaming for a position that probably requires filling water coolers, running to the coffee shop and making photocopies. That's not worth your time, unless you have a special interest in seeing how such companies function from the inside out.

We won't consider apprenticeships because they typically focus on technical trades like blacksmithing, electrical work or carpentry. There's nothing wrong with pursuing one of these careers, but apprenticeships typically lead directly to full-time technical work. College is the focus here. If you find an opportunity to apprentice under a graphic designer with CP-overlap potential, then we'll call it an internship for our purposes.

Small enterprise internships are your best bet for a number of reasons.

1. **The D.I.Y. (Do It Yourself) Factor.** Most small enterprises need your help, but they don't have the budget or know-how to go looking for an unpaid intern. By knocking on the door, saying "Hi, I like what you do, and I want to help...there are a few specific things I want to learn, but my first priority is assisting your business in any way I can," you're able to custom-design your internship from the start. Such a feat of creativity is very difficult in highly structured big business internships.

2. **Flexible scheduling.** Big internships and apprenticeships typically come with rigid schedules. Will a mandatory 10AM–2PM work schedule, every weekday for three months, necessarily fit with your other unschooling adventures? The key here is to obtain flexibility both in weekly scheduling and time off. A small enterprise will be more willing to shift weekly hours to accommodate your Spanish tutoring or two weeks off to travel in Belize. Find internships that embrace the results-oriented (and time-flexible) work ethic.

3. **Bigger responsibilities.** Small business owners often take on the multiple big responsibilities of owning a business (e.g. research and design, marketing, financial records, web design) all on their own. Large companies, while perhaps more sophisticated and established, are also more fragmented in their job duties. As an unschooler and an intern, you're looking to learn as much as possible, and that comes with being given bigger, wider responsibilities. Small enterprises will provide more opportunity to dip your paws into multiple pots of honey.

Crafting Your Internship

There are two factors for success in an internship. The first is getting your foot in the door, and the second is doing a good job once you're in. We're not going to discuss the second factor. Because an internship is essentially an unpaid job, you probably already have a network of experts (anyone who has worked in the type of company you'd like to join) who can advise you in how to be a strong worker. Let's tackle the first hurdle: getting your foot in the door, and if the door doesn't exist, how to craft one yourself.

1. **Start with your dream map.** Look at the bubbles on your dream map and ask yourself who does what I want to do, for money? Using the example dream map from Chapter 1, we find that the following people on the map make money doing things.

- Personal chefs cook four-course Italian dinners.
- Restaurant cooks work in local restaurants.
- Factory workers and owners build hybrid cars.
- Some auto shops convert diesel trucks to veggie oil.
- Hostel owners host international travelers.
- Political parties raise money for presidential candidates.
- Newspaper editors research and write political articles.

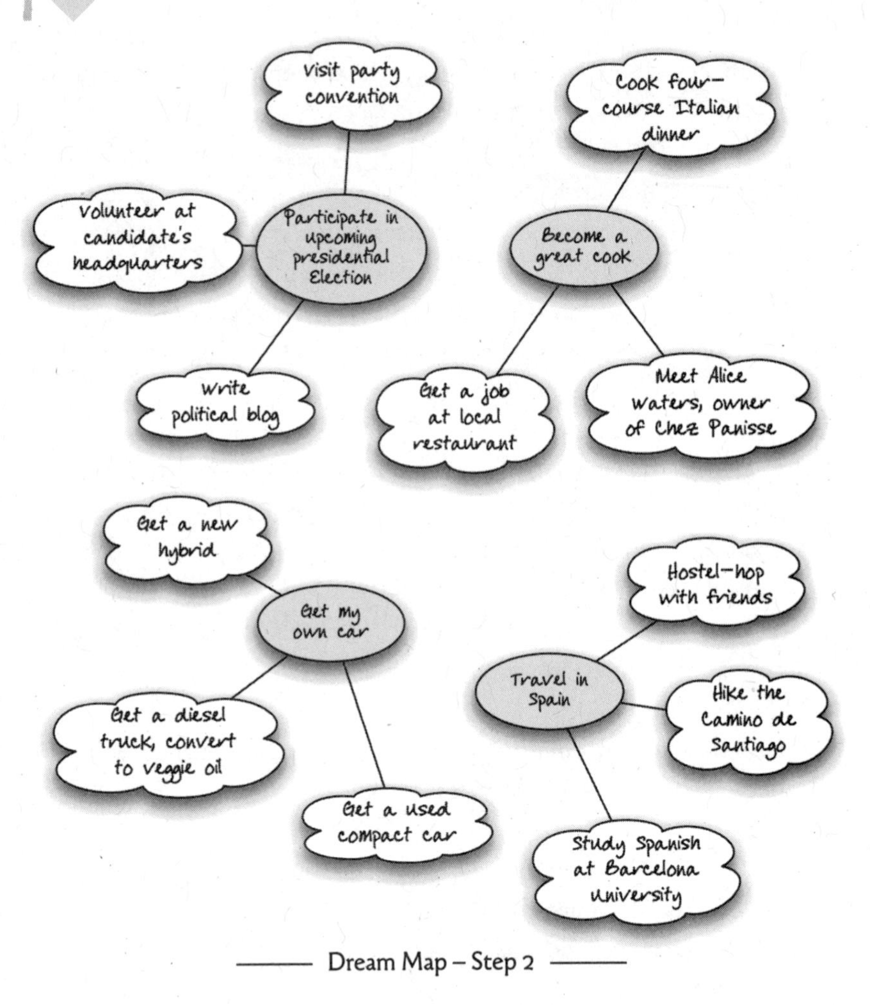

Dream Map – Step 2

2. **Apply the small enterprise criteria.** Which of the categories that you outlined fall under small enterprise? A company with fewer than 100 employees might technically be considered small. But I recommend aiming for those with 10 or fewer employees to maximize small enterprise benefits. So, professions matching our criteria include

- personal chefs
- restaurant cooks

- veggie oil-converting auto shops
- hostel owners
- political parties (depending on the size of the local chapter)
- newspaper editors (depending on the size of the paper)

(The car factory was the only one that got knocked out. With thousands of workers, getting a custom-fit internship there would be tough. Consider instead touring the factory or interviewing the hybrid vehicle engineers. See Hunting Down Heroes and Experts later in this chapter.)

3. **Find local enterprises.** Start with online yellow pages or a Google search. Use short search phrases like Santa Barbara veggie oil conversion (instead of browsing specific auto shops) that may lead you, for instance, to local SVO (straight vegetable oil) enthusiasts who have converted their own cars. These are the types of people who can lead you to local businesses that don't have an Internet presence. Restaurants and newspapers would be easy to find, but remember: easy means lots of competition. Searching out the hidden few private chefs in your area will prove more lucrative an internship opportunity than simply trying the restaurant down the street.

4. **Outline your goals and a trial period.** Do this *before* making contact. No serious business owner wants to spend more than 20 seconds with a walk-in teenager, especially if your intro line is, "I think I'd like to intern here...um, I don't know for how long...no, I don't really know what I want to do."

   Come up with three to five specific learning targets for your internship. These should be things that the company *does*, i.e., targets they can actually fulfill. If you're shooting for a veggie oil conversion internship, research the company online or call and ask for an explanation of their services.

Next, choose a specific number of days or weeks to propose as your internship trial period (one to two weeks is a good bet). This is vitally important as it gives the business an out if they feel that your internship is not worth their time. And this gives you a chance to get your foot in the door for a few weeks and show them your interest-driven energy. Proposing a longer-term internship will be substantially easier after a trial period.

5. **Now it's time to take the plunge**—here's where the fun starts. With internship goals and trial period length written on paper, call the company to pitch your internship idea. For reference, follow this sample conversation script between you, the prospective intern, and Green Overhauls (GO) auto shop, a fictional enterprise.

GO: Hello, Green Overhauls. Roger speaking.

You: Hi Roger.[1] My name is Ingrid and I'm interested learning about veggie oil conversions. With whom may I speak[2] to discuss volunteering or job shadowing opportunities[3] with your company?

GO: Oh, well, that would be Mary in the office. Hold on a second.

GO: Hello, this is Mary.

You: Hello Mary, my name is Ingrid. I'm a 16-year-old homeschooling student[4] and I'm very interested in alternative fuels and veggie oil in particular. My dream is to convert my own diesel truck to veggie oil and drive it across the country. I'm calling to discuss internship opportunities with your company.

GO: Well...we've never really had any interns, Ingrid. We're a very small company, you know, with four shop employees and two in the office. What exactly did you have in mind?[5]

You: Well Mary, I'm most interested in learning three things: how to physically perform a conversion, how to find clean sources of veggie oil and background on the alternative energy movement from people who are directly involved in it. But my first priority is to help your company. I can grab tools, staple papers, answer the phone or do whatever else you need.[6] And we could try it for two weeks at first with no commitment on your part.

GO: Interesting. You've thought this through, haven't you? Well you could certainly learn all those skills here at the shop, and we can always use help with the little tasks. Why don't you come in and talk with me and Ethan, the owner? Will tomorrow at 4:00 PM work for you?

This is the best-case scenario. But what if you're flatly turned down? Turn failure into opportunity by asking for a reference.

GO: Thank you for calling, Ingrid, but we really don't have the resources for taking on another person right now, not even a job shadow. We're simply swamped. Try back next year.

You: Thank you for your time anyway, Mary. Before we hang up, can you refer me to any other auto shops that do veggie oil conversions in the area that I might get in touch with? I'm really excited to make this internship happen.

6. **Prepare for the interview.** Dress cleanly, speak with confidence, make eye contact and reinforce your desire to learn. Remember that interviewers will probably pay special attention to your status as an unschooler. Make the company realize that

your unschooling is to their benefit; it means that you're more flexible with scheduling, more self-motivated and more available for a long-term commitment.

7. **Rock the interview.** And you're in.

If your local area doesn't provide enough options for the type of internship you seek, consider using an internship placement service. One of the oldest and best is the Center for Interim Programs. The Center does one-on-one consulting (for a fee) with teens who seek internships and other experiential programs in specific interest areas.[7]

CP Batching Potential

Internships are superstars of batching potential. Use them to

- demonstrate **Intellectual Passion** by showing that you've gained abstract knowledge from real world work. For every thousand teens who read about alternative fuels and write an impassioned environmentalist essay, only one will brew an alternative fuel herself. Production (instead of mere consumption) shows passion.
- show **Background Knowledge** by keeping a list of tasks accomplished during the internship and getting it signed by your supervisor. Include both hands-on and intellectual accomplishments (e.g. Converted Mercedes-Benz to straight veggie oil; Studied pressure-temperature relation inside engine pistons.).
- show **Leadership** by noting internship responsibilities on your résumé.

International Volunteering

Want to teach basic computer skills in Tanzania? Protect turtle egg hatcheries in Costa Rica? Tutor English at an elementary school in

Peru (and surf every day, on the side)? If so, international volunteering is for you.

What's wrong with international travel or volunteering by themselves, you might ask? For the first case, make no mistake: traveling internationally, either solo or with a small group, is the quintessential adventure. International travel rips you out of every comfort zone and drops you in a land with different language, food, money and social customs. As a learning experience, it is unparalleled.

But independent travel is expensive, relatively risky as a teen and demands a level of street smarts that most young people (even unschoolers) gain only in their late teens or early 20s. You can get into serious trouble traveling in any country (developed or developing) by yourself. For these reasons, I don't recommend independent international travel unless you're going with an experienced partner or group.

Volunteering, on the other end of the spectrum, is far too easy as most teens know it. Delivering Christmas presents to the needy, picking up trash and babysitting may feel good for a while, but they're not all-encompassing learning experiences. Organizing fundraisers for the Red Cross gets old fast without an extra element of challenge.

The solution to overambitious travel and unchallenging volunteering is to combine the two. Do your volunteering in a land far, far away, in a language you don't (yet) understand, and suddenly it becomes an adventure.

Volunteering and international travel make good bedfellows for the teenage traveler for two reasons. Firstly, most international volunteering positions for teens include a home stay. Instead of wandering alone across the seas (to the horror of your parents' imagination), you're under the wings of a screened host family. And secondly, volunteering provides a physical and mental home base from which to strike out. Not having to worry about lodging, food and transportation removes a large and potentially stressful aspect of international travel from your hands, freeing you to focus on more important matters (like meeting other travelers or doing your volunteer work).

The Volunteer Vacation Warning

A hundred companies exist that will build you a custom-length volunteering position, complete with home stay, airport transfer and language lessons—for $3000–6000.

These volunteer vacations take all the hassle out of international volunteering, and unfortunately, most of the challenge too. Pre-packaged trips such as these are no longer adventures but exactly what they call themselves: vacations. And suddenly you're paying thousands of dollars to do volunteer work.

I recommend spending the extra hours online to find low-cost international volunteering projects. Many projects will pay for your room and board if you commit for a certain period of time. And a few opportunities are 100% free; one South American volunteer website[8] listed opportunities to study wildcats, lead horse packing trips, teach surfing and skateboarding and learn coastal oil spill rehabilitation with no program or room and board fees.

Search hard for your volunteering opportunity, and don't accept the first volunteer vacation that falls into your lap.

If you're still wary of foreign travel, know that the word international can effectively mean far away in the United States. You don't have to leave the country. But remember that new languages and culture shock create the all-inclusive adventure that we're shooting for here. If you're going to volunteer within the US or Canada, choose a position far removed from your day-to-day life. If you're from California, consider Alabama or Quebec. If you're from Alabama or Quebec, consider California.

How to Do It

1. **Begin with interests, not needs.** The world yearns for knowledgeable volunteers to teach English, build water systems, lead health workshops and serve a hundred other noble causes. Remember, however, that you're volunteering to *learn hands-on* about a subject of *your* interest. Your first priority is to select a project that matches your dream maps. Serving the neediest is a generic that will take you only so far, because guilt is a poor motivator.

2. **Start on Idealist.org.** Of the dozens of websites offering international volunteer programs, Idealist.org is the most established and reputable. Browse the Volunteer Opportunities section of the site, and limit your search to the teenage age range. You can also browse country-by-country or by area of focus (e.g. disaster relief, health and medicine). Even if Idealist.org doesn't have the right project for you, it can grease your creative gears for a more general online search.

3. **Google specific projects.** Take interesting project ideas, harvested from Idealist.org or elsewhere, and paste them into a Google search. If restoring ancient castles in France is your interest, use those words, but also include the words volunteer, home stay and teen. Steer immediately away from packages asking for fees beyond reasonable room, board and transportation costs.

4. **Call to verify existence.** Volunteer opportunities that look good online may have dried up like puddles in the sun since they

were posted. Before investing in an application or cover letter, call the project's contact number and confirm its existence. Use Skype[9] to make ultra-low-cost phone calls from your computer to any international number.

5. **Confirm details, examine applications and tackle age restrictions.** Armed with a handful of existence-verified international volunteering possibilities, pore in-depth into the details and applications of each prospective project. Write e-mails to project coordinators and ask for all application materials, dates, fees and host family backgrounds. Some volunteering positions have firm 18+ age limits, and it's good to learn that as quickly as possible. Many more projects will simply require a signature from your parents indicating their legal approval of your participation; you may have to suggest this idea.

6. **Get references.** This is the most important step. Ask for the names and e-mails of two to four current or past volunteers. Get in touch with these people and ask every question in your brain before seriously considering *any* project.

7. **Money, money, money.** Unless you're financially independent, international volunteering will require fundraising or help from your parents. Costs will include airfare ($500–$1500 roundtrip for most places in the world), program fees and living expenses.

   Because the initial costs of travel add up quickly, you'll get much more value if you choose a longer trip (two+ months) and avoid totally modernized areas like Western Europe or New Zealand. Take for example my 2007 trip through South America. Staying in backpackers' hostels and eating out every meal, I comfortably traveled on $1000 per month in Peru, Bolivia and Argentina. With $800 round-trip airfare from

California, if I had stayed for only two weeks, my total price would have been \$800 (air) + \$500 (½ month of travel) = \$1300. That's a rate of \$2600 per month. But I stayed for three months, paying \$800 (air) + \$3000 (travel) = \$3800. That's a rate of less than \$1300 per month, or more than twice the value factor of the shorter trip. The same math applies to volunteering abroad: longer trips pay off.

8. **Get your passport, get your shots and get out of here!** Don't underestimate the wrath of the post office (where you apply for a passport). Passport regulations can change and create massive application backups, forcing unlucky applicants to wait six+ months before leaving the country. Get your passport now. Check the State Department traveler's website for a database of recommended vaccinations and safety warnings for specific countries.[10] Like passports, begin vaccinations early as some multi-shot treatments may demand months.

Another Option: International Farm Work

Why consider volunteering internationally on a farm? Grace Llewellyn put it best.

> Getting involved with the lives of the plants and animals that we eat fills a big gap in our "educations," a gap the schools can't possibly fill. The field trip to look at cows doesn't cut it. Nor does the photograph of cornfields on page 361 of your American Heritage book, or chopping up rats in biology... No one ever argues convincingly against the goodness of contact with the fundamental building blocks our lives.[11]

The preeminent organization for finding international farm work is WWOOF: World Wide Opportunities on Organic Farms. Dozens of countries have their own WWOOF organization, each of whom publishes an annual directory of farming opportunities; purchasing or accessing these directories online costs roughly $20.

WWOOF is an unschooler's dream. Host families provide housing and meals (straight from the farm) in exchange for four-six hours of daily labor. Because you make arrangements directly with the host families, you can skirt the age regulations that typically come with paid programs. And because the host farm doesn't technically pay you anything, you can live on a tourist visa, which leaves you ample time to explore your country after finishing the WWOOF term.

CP Batching Potential

Here are a few ways to batch international volunteering.

- Show Intellectual Passion by supplementing, as with internships, your academic interests with hands-on knowledge.
- Show Background Knowledge in a foreign language by learning it posthaste via cultural immersion.
- Show Leadership simply through the fact that you volunteered, in another country, without defaulting to the volunteer vacation. This is incredibly impressive in itself.

Hunting Down Heroes and Experts

> Framingham, Massachusetts—The giant stone mansion looks just like the photographs. Children dash across sprawling green lawns under the New England spring sun. I walk a twisting asphalt footpath to the Sudbury Valley School: the first and largest US free school and the focus of two years of my independent study in college. The school's founders agreed to let me visit, a privilege denied to virtually all outsiders in recent years. I should be basking in my fortune, but all I'm thinking is, Are they going to scream at me?
>
> I suppose plagiarism isn't the best way to say hello.

Earlier that year I decided to make the grandest college course reader (textbook made from photocopies) ever known to humanity. It was for Never Taught to Learn, an undergraduate education course that I had started. The reader, resembling royal parchment on its oversized and spiral-bound paper, included excerpts from every major unschooling-friendly author, including those of one of the founders of the Sudbury Valley School.

To produce this masterpiece, I did what every college professor does: photocopy directly from the author's books to create my reader. With only 12 students in my tiny class, I assumed that some vague notion of academic freedom protected me from any potential legal qualms of photocopying, oh, ¾ of one of the SVS books. That assumption was my big mistake.

Four weeks into the class I received an unsolicited e-mail from the one of the school's founders with a single line of content: "Blake, I noticed that you're using some of our books in your course reader. Would you please tell me exactly which books and how many pages you're using?" Woops—I guess I shouldn't have posted the course syllabus online. Defaulting to honesty as the best medicine, I wrote him back with the exact numbers.

The next day I received a scathing e-mail from another one of the school's founders. She accused me (rightfully) of plagiarizing the school's books and demanded royalties and an immediate apology. It was a slap to my face to realize that I'd committed intellectual theft, but I admitted my mistake, stayed up all night writing an apology letter and mailed it the next day with an $80 royalty check.

Slipped into the end of my apology letter I included a humble question. "I photocopied your books because I deeply admire your school," I wrote, "and I would cherish the opportunity to see it in person." It was a shot in the dark for an opportunity I assumed I'd already ruined.

To my utter surprise, I received a response by e-mail only a week later. The staff had read my letter, were touched and grudgingly decided to allow me a one-day visit. What authors, reporters and graduate students had consistently been denied—a full day visit to the country's oldest free school—I had just been granted.

Three months later I found myself walking down that twisted asphalt path, circled by cartwheeling free schoolers, wondering if this was a booby trap. But I wasn't executed in the dungeons of Sudbury Valley. I shook the founders' hands and spent a fantastic day soaking up Sudbury's unstructured, democratic school culture. I met my heroes and the experts of the free school movement.

But there are better ways to do it.

—The Author

What makes hunting down a hero or expert an adventure? You're not ducking waterfalls in New Zealand or shadowing a kidney operation, after all. It's just a little phone call.

First, that little phone call is extremely hard to make. Try to get a professional sports player or recent best-selling author on the phone, and you'll experience the novel feeling of being totally shut down ("No, he won't talk with you").

Secondly, the potential knowledge payoff of contacting a hero or expert is huge. Doing research totally on one's own is often difficult, and spending too much time researching the wrong question can be demoralizing. Finding a mind that can point you, without hesitation, to the best learning resources (such as books, names, websites and enterprises) in your specific area will catapult your self-directed research to new heights.

What does hunting down a hero or expert look like? Let's consider a fictional unschooler, Rebecca.

Robots fascinate Rebecca. She has absorbed tons of information about robot theory (e.g. intelligence programming) and robotics (the design and building of robots), but now she's hit a mental plateau. Her research seems to be repeating itself, and she wants to take it to the next level. To continue her quest, Rebecca decides to investigate the nearby research university for a knowledgeable robot expert to guide her.

Searching the university website, Rebecca discovers a Robotics research group consisting of two professors, four graduate students and a handful of undergraduate assistants. Looking over the member biographies, Rebecca chooses one graduate student and one undergraduate whose interests best match her own and notes their e-mails, office locations and office phone numbers. Who to try first? Rebecca realizes that the grad students are more knowledgeable but also more busy, and undergraduates the opposite. She decides to be a bit unreasonable and try first for the graduate student.

Rebecca has three contact options: e-mail, phone and office. As a teenager and unschooler, Rebecca realizes that she runs the risk of being misunderstood if she doesn't have a chance to explain her educational philosophy. An e-mail or voicemail might just get deleted. Her best chance to meet this expert, she decides, is to walk right into his office. Grad students, like professors, typically have office hours during which they hang around and wait for undergraduates to show up with questions. Most undergraduates seldom use office hours. Rebecca finds her graduate student's scheduled office hours online, and shows up then to make her move. Walking into the office, Rebecca introduces herself.

*Rebecca (R): *Knock Knock**
Graduate Student (GS): Hello, may I help you?

R: Hi, my name is Rebecca. Are you Alex?

GS: Yes, I'm Alex. What can I do for you, Rebecca? Are you a student here?

R: No, I'm a homeschooler. Actually, I'm an unschooler, which means I design most of my own learning. I'm really interested in robotics, and saw your work with the research group online. I was hoping to ask you a few quick questions to help me in my own research.

GS: Well, yes, I suppose I can help. I have a student coming in 15 minutes—can we be done by then?

R: Of course. [Pulling a paper pad with notes out of her backpack] Can we start with biomechanics? I'd love to know where to start in finding out...

R: (15 minutes later) Thanks Alex, you've been a huge help. May I keep in touch with you via e-mail or the occasional phone call with future questions?

Rebecca walks away from her 15-minute interview with a list of high-quality books, videos, websites and enterprises to explore and the phone numbers of three other graduate students to contact with additional questions. With this network of contacts, she has set the foundation for finding the best resources for her robotics interest. The hunt was successful.

Starting your own hunt

1. **Find potential targets.** If you already have a certain target in mind, great. If not, use the following list as brain fodder. Which experts may potentially have answers to the questions you're looking for?

- Authors
- Newspaper columnists
- Blog writers
- Small enterprise owners and managers

- Business professionals
- College graduate students (Masters and Ph.D. candidates)
- College undergraduate students
- College groups, clubs and talent organizations
- College professors
- Non-university researchers (e.g. think tanks, policy research organizations)

2. **Turn interests into questions.** Like Rebecca, you can show your target that you're serious by being ready with specific, prepared questions. The more talented an expert, the busier she will be, and the less time she'll have for vague, undefined queries. Choose three goals from your dream map and write them in bubbles on a piece of scratch paper. Expand each bubble into three to five specific questions that you find compelling.

3. **Do your homework.** Now that you have potential experts and potential questions, find out where they overlap. Research your targets' writings, research, successes and failures. Googling her name will usually take care of this. This step is important because when you meet your target, you'll have a scant few moments to convince her that she won't need to reinvent the wheel for you—i.e., that you're basically familiar with the research that gives her expert status.

4. **Walk in, call or e-mail.** These options are listed in order of preference.

   Walking in (to an office or business) is the best way to get around gatekeepers. Most adults are surprised to see a teen in their workplace, and they'll grant you a meeting simply out of curiosity of your motives. If your hero or expert lives far away, your best option is to call. E-mails are useful as supplements, but not replacements, for the all-important walk-in or phone call.

When calling or walking in, prepare an introduction. This is a four-part paragraph explaining (1) who you are, (2) what you know, (3) what you want to know and (4) how long it will take. For example: "Hi, my name is ________, and I'm a homeschooling student. I'm familiar with [one or two specific pieces of your target's research]. I was hoping to get your input on two quick questions regarding [subject] in my personal research. This will take less than 10 minutes of your time."

5. **Be brief, and ask for a follow-up.** A true expert's time is always in short supply, so be brief. Get in, introduce yourself, ask your questions and get out. *Tell* her that you know her time is valuable and then act on it. To build a bridge for future follow-up (that's the goal, after all), ask permission to call or e-mail (low-commitment communication) in the future.

6. **Write a thank-you, and follow up as promised.** It sounds hokey, but a thank-you note will help make or break your future hero-expert relationship. E-mail (or write a real letter) thanking your target for her time and expertise, and say that you're excited to continue your relationship in the future. Within one week, ask a follow-up or clarification question—even if you don't need to. This will reinforce the relationship you started one week ago, ensuring a solid foundation for future questions that pop into your head a week, month or year later.

Crashing a College Course

If you live close to a four-year college, a unique opportunity for taking advantage of a friendly expert presents itself: the opportunity to crash a college course.

Crashing, in traditional college lingo, means going to the first meeting of class (without being enrolled in that class) in the hopes of taking the spot of an enrolled student who doesn't show up. This isn't our definition. Crashing a college course in the unschooler's lingo means attending and participating in a class without being enrolled.

We previously discussed auditing college classes as a CP result. Auditing is a fine choice, if your local college offers it. But if auditing is not an official option, consider crashing as an alternative.

College courses come in two broad flavors: lower-division and upper-division. Lower-division courses, typically taken by freshmen and sophomores, are large, introductory-level and lecture-based. A first-year biology course at a public university, for example, may have 300 students in the lecture hall. These courses break up into smaller groups—perhaps around 15 students—for weekly discussion sections. Upper-division courses, in contrast, are typically taken by juniors and seniors. They are smaller, more specialized, and (while still lecture-based) heavier in classroom discussion.

As a teenage unschooler, crashing a lower-division course is your best bet. In the largest freshman courses (my own alma mater, UC Berkeley, has an introductory calculus course enrolling roughly 800 students), crashing lectures is easy: simply walk in and listen. Few such courses take roll, and most students keep to themselves. Your presence won't disturb anyone. You can do this by yourself, with an unschooling accomplice or with an undergraduate friend (who you met using the techniques discussed above for hunting down heroes and experts).

But what if a fascinating lower-division course has only 50 students, making you more visible? Or what if you want to participate in a weekly discussion sections in which roll is taken?

Each college course has its gatekeepers. For the types of courses that we're discussing, the gatekeepers are typically graduate students (often called teaching assistants). Unbeknownst to college-bound teens, most college professors do not manage their (lower-division) classes; graduate students take roll, run discussions and grade homework and tests. The professor shows up, lectures and then gets back to her own research. The key to crashing a smaller course therefore lies in the course's gatekeepers: the graduate student teaching assistants.

To crash a smaller course or discussion section, follow Rebecca's example and initiate a relationship with a graduate student who runs the course in which you're interested. Then pop the question. A friendly and supportive graduate student ally may even add you to the official course roster, giving you a powerful Structured Learning result.

CP Batching Potential

Use your relationships with heroes and experts to

- Show ***Intellectual Passion***. Tracking down heroes is the quintessential act of the intellectually passionate.
- Show ***Background Knowledge*** and ***Logical Reasoning*** by demonstrating your working relationship with experts in an academic field.
- Show ***Leadership*** through your initiative in building relationships with strangers.
- Show ***Structured Learning*** by participating in college courses as an auditor or crasher.

Business Start-Up

Ask any adult who has done it. Starting your own business is an undeniable adventure, often fun and always a learning experience. As a talented teen with a liberated schedule and few expenses (assuming you're still under your parents' wing), you're well positioned to dedicate time to a business start-up.

There are two general types of businesses: product and service. In a product business, you stock and sell physical items (think: a clothing store or cafe). In a service business, you sell a human service (think: graphic design or massage).

Product business makes sense for unschoolers who are master handcrafters or experts in a niche market. India, a 17-year-old unschooler in Northern California, creates small dolls that she sells at farmers' markets. If you've been involved with physical therapy rehabilitation, perhaps you have sufficient expertise to build ergonomic devices for people with tendonitis.

But if you're not a master builder, my advice is to forget about product businesses. Purchasing inventory costs a lot of money (e.g., a $400 investment in blank t-shirts for your shirt design company), and online marketplaces make competition stiff. Service businesses, in contrast, require virtually zero start-up costs and are inherently local (you can't give a massage over the Internet).

Good advice for starting your own service business abounds in the business section of your local bookstore, library or free online. Use these resources, but don't get overwhelmed when you start reading sections about taxes, licenses and all the other legalities that convince most teens that they're not allowed to start a business. We'll drive over each of those speed bumps in due time.

Growing Your (Service) Business Adventure

1. **Begin with your unschooling (interest-driven) talents.** Each of these talents encompasses a potential service.

2. **Realize that expertise is relative.** Just because you don't have an official expert title in your skill doesn't mean your business must die in embryo. The term expert is relative to the client. If you have more knowledge and talent in an area than the client, then you're effectively a helpful expert as far as their needs are concerned.

   As a 16-year-old tutor and web designer, I was by no means an official algebra expert or web design professional. But I knew more about algebra than my 13-year-old tutee and more about websites than my dad (my first client). Thus, I was a relative expert.

3. **Write your main benefit in one sentence.** This step wraps together three vital business start-up moves: defining your market, separating yourself from competition and crafting a mission statement. I'm a big fan of keeping business planning to a minimum, because you'll get your best feedback from customers when you start actually offering your service. In other words: trust your talent and keep planning to a minimum to avoid analysis paralysis.

   Why should I spend my hard-earned dollars on your service? This is the question that you're answering in one sentence. More than likely, you were a consumer of the service that you're selling before you became a provider; put yourself in the client's shoes and ask if you would hire yourself. Don't imagine yourself as a mythical customer with dollars to burn on helping out or giving a chance to young entrepreneurs. Imagine that (like most adults) you have a very limited budget and want the absolute best value you can find, no matter who the seller is.

   Do you bake killer organic brownies? Write in one sentence why the local café, community center and natural foods grocery should buy yours instead of a commercial variety.

   Blake's brownies use 100% organic ingredients, including extra dark organic chocolate, and are delivered fresh-baked to your door within 48 hours.

   Can you teach your natural-material arts and crafts skill to young children? Write in one sentence why spending an afternoon with leaves, sticks, flowers, glue and colored paper is a better choice for a parent's children than daycare or television.

Amelia's Afternoon Crafts gives children ages 4–7 an outdoor alternative to daycare, building awareness of the natural world and making art an everyday joy.

Ready to take your violin skills to the next level—public performance? Write in one sentence why a dinner party, fundraiser or wedding reception should hire you over a more experienced (and expensive) violinist or no performer at all.

Recitals by Casey adds the elegant touch of classical music to your small event for half the price of the competition.

Notice how the one-sentence benefit borders on an advertising pitch? That's what we're going for. When a prospective client asks about your service, you have roughly seven seconds to capture their attention; having a condensed summary sentence ready will capture that attention and show professionalism.

4. **Write a FAQ list.** Keep a FAQ (Frequently Asked Questions) list on hand every time you interact with a potential client (over the phone or e-mail), and post it on your website if you have one. Start by writing down answers to every question that you think will be commonly asked (Are your brownies baked safely? Have you cared for children before? Do you have music samples?). Then, after you begin offering your service, add the questions which pop up in the course of business (What type of flour do you use?) to the list.

5. **Advertise for free (or cheap) with flyers, Craigslist and pay-per-click.** First, a warning: paid advertising in any form is always inferior to the most powerful marketing tool on earth,

word-of-mouth. Three positive references from satisfied customers can be worth more than $3000 in advertising.

Paper flyers are your first choice for making your local community aware of your business offerings. Start with public bulletin boards at coffee shops, libraries, grocery stores and community centers to target the general public. If your service is in a niche market, then focus further advertising on where that market gathers (e.g., advertise Judo instruction in gyms). Always ask business management before posting a flier (unless public posting is specifically allowed)—often you'll need a timestamp or other (free) mark of approval to ensure the flyer's survival.

Online advertising is the next step. Start with free advertising on Craigslist by posting an ad in the services section.[12] Then do a Google search for online classifieds in your local area and put up your free ad there.

Finally, an easy, cheap and effective form of online paid advertising that you can dabble with is pay-per-click (PPC).

In the early days of the Internet, advertisers would pay for banner space—a permanent or rotating ad on a certain web page. This worked like magazine advertising, where you could target a certain group (e.g., horror movie aficionados) but had little idea of how many people were actually acting on your advertisement. PPC differs in that you only pay for advertising when someone clicks on your ad. The click then directs the person to your website (which can be easily built and hosted online for free, if you're up to the challenge of learning web design). PPC ads typically show up on the right side of a user's web browser, as anyone familiar with Google's services will know.

PPC ads, in combination with local flyers, online classifieds and the ever-powerful word-of-mouth reference, will begin to the process of taking your business idea from fantasy to reality.

6. **Get business cards for free.** I don't believe in spending lots of time and money creating a professional image if you aren't in fact a professional, but business cards can be found for nearly free online—and they look pretty awesome. Google free business cards or try Vista Print, which offered totally free cards (plus shipping & handling) as of 2009.[13]

7. **Offer your service!** This is the part where you exchange goods and services for money.

8. **Don't sweat the official stuff until you start making money.** Realistically speaking, your small service business requires no official registration with state authorities. Millions of informal service-business transactions take place every day (babysitting, lawn-mowing, web design) that are *supposed* to be reported to the IRS, but they're not. The IRS is not going to track down your violin recital service until you start doing $1000 performances. Up until that point, don't worry too much about being official.

   When you do go official, you'll likely form a sole proprietorship or limited liability company (LLC). These are both very easy to form, so don't let the fancy words scare you off. Learn more about each online and in the business section of bookstores and libraries.

CP Batching Potential

Starting your own business can

- Show ***Leadership***, because business start-up takes incredible determination and initiative (especially if you manage employees).

- Show *Intellectual Passion*. Colleges are enthused to admit a student with business knowledge of their academic area (like a prospective nutritionist who analyzes the vitamin content of his organic brownies or the prospective child psychology major who runs her own after school program).

Community Skill Mastery

Unschoolers often fly solo in their ventures because the pace of learning in high school classrooms is simply too slow. But there is much learning to be gained in community—not a forced community like high school, but a community of choice like a group or practice club.

Learning in community has the potential to be extremely effective because you surround yourself with people who are both passionate and talented in your same area of interest. And when communities from across a region gather to form retreats, conferences, seminars, trainings and competitions, the passion and talent really flows. Events like these—opportunities for community skill mastery—are big-time adventures.

Sixteen-year-old unschooler Brenna McBroom describes NaNoWriMo, an online community competition for aspiring fiction writers.

> In 2005 my interest in writing had faltered. Making excuses for not writing had slowly replaced writing as my hobby. Soon after that, like a gift from the literary gods, I discovered an online competition called NaNoWriMo (National Novel Writing Month). I entered my name into the database, signing myself up to write a 50,000-word novel in 30 days.
>
> The competition ran the entire month of November. At one minute after midnight on November 1st, with no plan (and certainly no plot), I plunked myself down at my computer keyboard and began crafting my masterpiece. Four stressful

and exhilarating weeks later, I finally put the last period on the last sentence of my completed, 50,000-word novel.

Forcing myself to string together 1,667 words every day for a month was ideal. As an aspiring writer, I'm very good at making up things I think I need before I start writing. "I need to take a writing class." "I need to buy a good pen and a hardbound journal." "I need inspiration and life experience." Sometimes classes and pens and self-discovery trips to Europe are helpful, but they're usually nothing more than excuses for procrastination. NaNoWriMo gave me exactly what I needed: a swift kick in the pants forcing me to write.

Writing often still seems like a chore, but I took something away from NaNoWriMo that helps me even when I feel like I'd rather eat a bowl of ants than work on my newest poem or think about my college admissions essay for one more second: the knowledge that in order to be a better writer, I had to stop "getting ready to write" and just start writing.

To find your own community skill mastery adventure, seek out any place where lots of people gather to practice, preach, refine or debate a specific talent, skill or set of ideas. These typically include

- Retreats
- Conferences
- Competitions
- Summer seminars/camps
- Community classes/groups
- Paid trainings

1. **Begin with an Internet search combining your interest/hobby/talent with one of the above words.** For example, if you're fascinated by Project SETI (the Search for ExtraTerrestrial Intelligence), Google SETI retreat, SETI conference or SETI camp.

2. **Look for volunteer opportunities at large-scale events like professional conferences and national competitions.** These are your best (and cheapest) bets for getting into events that others pay thousands of dollars to attend. Remember that few volunteer opportunities will be listed online, and event organizers can always use an extra pair of hands. Using the guidelines for tracking down heroes and experts earlier in this chapter, contact event organizers, explain your age and passion and tell that that you'd love to help out in any way.

3. **For wider/undefined interests, include your city name in the search.** If you're a writer, this will find your local writer's groups (who can likely connect you to things like writer's retreats and conferences). A search for poverty, conference and Michigan finds you dozens of speeches, meetings, groups and conferences in the Michigan area about global poverty. The more narrowly that you define your interests (e.g., SETI data analysis), the more you'll need to travel to reach specialized and infrequent events. The pay-off comes in superior expertise and networking opportunities.

4. **Look for opportunities to gain certification in your area.** Get your pilot's license in your quest to learn physics. Become an Emergency Medical Technician to begin your study of human anatomy. Take community college classes for Early Childhood Education units to kick-start your child psychology research. Certification can open doors to adventures like starting your own business, getting internships and meeting experts in addition to the contacts you make in the certification training itself.

5. **Search Craiglist.org for community groups and classes.** Did you know that the family next-door likes to geocache (search for

hidden treasures with GPS devices)? I didn't either. Craigslist and other community websites can help you find community learning opportunities a short walk, bike or drive away.

CP Batching Potential

Use your community skill mastery experiences to show Leadership, Background Knowledge and Intellectual Passion. These experiences typically pay off more in social networking than in CP results.

Making the Leap

Final Notes on the Unschooling Decision

Monica Chen had it all.

In her junior year at a hyper-competitive Silicon Valley public high school, Monica was an AP-and-Honors student with high grades. Her college preparatory accomplishment list included membership in multiple academic clubs and over 100 community service hours. On the fast track to prestigious universities like many of her classmates, Monica Chen had it all—but something was missing.

High school was sucking up every moment of Monica's time as she worked furiously like a college preparatory machine. To get ahead in AP History, she skipped lunches to memorize note sheets in the hall. Her few remnants of personal time disappeared as projects and final exams pushed bedtime to 1:00, 2:00 or 3:00 AM. In literature class, with a grade of 110%, Monica laid her head on her desk in a moment of low-energy boredom. The teacher snapped, "Monica, what's wrong with you? At least fake it!" To save paper when printing an honors English report, Monica used double-sided formatting when the assignment called for single-sided. Her A paper dropped to a B, causing her more stress than any human should place on a single letter.

At the end of junior year Monica was totally exhausted. But it wasn't the satisfying exhaustion from running a race you choose—it was the dogged exhaustion of running on a wheel for a piece of cheese hanging always an inch away. Monica was only one year away from graduation and her promised college future when she asked herself, Why keep killing myself? Contemplating an Emerson quote ("We are always getting ready to live, but never living"), Monica looked inside and saw herself preparing to live...when? After high school? After college? After career and retirement and death?

Enough was enough. Monica left school that summer and began unschooling.

Immediately Monica's mental health improved as she initiated a heavy regiment of self-directed and interest-based activities. She started writing a daily blog, became an active member of environmental and social justice groups through the community college and fought to integrate organic foods choices into the cafeteria as a representative of the California Student Sustainability Coalition. On weekends she traveled to political protests and teach-ins around San Francisco. And because four-year college was still on the menu, Monica enrolled in economics, political science, psychology, film, environmental biology and calculus through her local community college to fulfill college prep requirements.

In the winter of her un-senior year, Monica applied to many of the same prestigious colleges that she was preparing for in her previous life. And nine months after her decision to skip senior year, Monica accepted enrollment at UC Berkeley. Doing what few other teens would brave, Monica left the high school track and ignored its threats of academic suicide. She had it all, and she gave it all up. And the world did not crumble.

Defining the Dropout Nightmare

> To do or not to do? To try or not to try? Most people will vote no, whether they consider themselves brave or not. Uncertainty and the prospect of failure can be very scary noises in the shadows. Most people will choose unhappiness over uncertainty.
>
> —Tim Ferriss[1]

Like wondering if you should get out of a warm bed teetering on a cliff, you may know that leaving school is what you *need* to do but don't *want* to do. Inertia is a powerful force that keeps many would-be unschoolers in soul-crushing school. Let's expose inertia for what it is. Ask yourself: what is the absolute worst that could happen if you left school?

Leaving school after her junior year, Monica could have been mocked as a lowly high school dropout and swiftly rejected by every prestigious college, relegating her to a life of dialing "Earn your degree from home!" numbers on late-night TV.

Halfway through my thoroughly impressive astrophysics major, I decided to design my own degree in Alternative Education Theory. This is a move akin to publishing a scientific paper on UFOs in the eyes of ivory tower researchers. What is the worst that could have happened to me with my major change? Well, my parents and friends could have lost all respect for me as an intelligent person. I could have thrown away 14 years of math and science study for some flowery free the children theories and ruined any serious career prospects. The professors sponsoring my major could have rejected my thesis paper as a piece of tripe, condemning me to another year of college that my parents wouldn't fund because they'd lost all respect for me. Damn.

But neither Monica's life, nor my own, met such a grim fate. Monica still went to college. I graduated from college, and neither of us lost respect in the eyes of people who cared about us. For most young adults who go about the unschooling decision in an organized and thoughtful way, success is the norm and regret the exception. Most fears appear ridiculous when you wrench them from the dark corners of your mind and examine them in the light of reality. The scary spider scaling your leg in the sleeping bag is almost always an ant.

Rock climbers understand safety in terms of *actual* risk and *perceived* risk. First-time climbers will become afraid of falling when they first climb ten feet above the ground. Of course, they are strapped into a belay system that can carry 1,500 pounds. While the perceived risk of falling is high, the actual risk is nearly zero. That same novice climber will drive home on the highway, weaving between trucks at 65 miles per hour, because driving is a perceived low-risk activity. Driving accidents cause tens of thousands of injuries and deaths every year (and this information is widely published), but because driving is *familiar*, it has a low perceived risk.

When you ask yourself what terrible fate may befall your decision to unschool, how much of that fear is perceived risk, and how much is actual risk? How many drug-addicted, burger-flipping, ignorant, bigoted and socially inept high school dropouts do you actually know? And does this stereotypical high school dropout leave school for the same reasons that you will: to actively pursue a life of learning and adventure?

Define your dropout nightmare. Envision your worst-case scenario in detail. And then ask: Could I repair this damage? Chances are that your old life is recoverable with a small investment of time and energy. What if no colleges accepted Monica because she skipped senior year? She could have taken a few semesters of community college and applied again as a junior transfer. What if my major change was a major flop? I could have switched back to astrophysics and taken out a loan to support myself for another year of college.

Now ask yourself a more important question: what is the cost of postponing action? In other words, what is the emotional, intellectual, physical or spiritual cost of burying your dreams? If you don't do what excites you today, where will you be in one year, five years or 20 years? Will you forgive yourself for sacrificing your biggest goals for the sake of inertia?

Don't blame bad timing. When big decisions are at stake, the timing is never right. Ninety-nine percent of the time, the real hesitation boils down to one word—*fear*. If the cost of inaction is high and your nightmare scenario is repairable, are you simply afraid of taking action? Let's finish our journey by killing the final few fears that may prevent you from taking the action you most need.

Meet Grace Llewellyn

The unschooling decision involves dozens of logistical questions. How do I homeschool legally in my state? How do I talk to my parents about unschooling? How do I join a sports team or get around town? Answering these questions is integral to dispelling the dropout nightmare.

I'm sorry to tell you that you won't find the full lexicon of unschooling questions-and-answers in this book. I would have addressed more of these questions if someone else hadn't already done it better.

In 1991, Grace Llewellyn, a former middle school English teacher, published *The Teenage Liberation Handbook: How to Quit School and Get a Real Life and Education*. The TLH, which became an instant underground classic, outlines in step-by-step detail how to

- Tackle homeschooling regulations, deal with school authorities and leave high school legally in all 50 states.[2]
- Talk to your parents about unschooling and win their vote of confidence.
- Take a de-schooling vacation to clear your mind and get ready for unschooling adventures.

- Deal with money and transportation, and build a social life without school.
- Find learning resources in science, math, social studies, English, foreign language and the arts (with numerous specific recommendations).
- Get started with volunteering, internships, jobs, farm work, social activism, outdoor travel, international travel, college and other adventures.

The handbook is fully worth its weight in inspiration, tactics and stories from real-life teenaged unschoolers, and it has helped thousands of teens conquer their fears of leaving school.[3]

Grace also runs Not Back to School Camp, a gathering for unschoolers ages 13–18. The camp has week-long sessions in Oregon and Vermont each year, and it is an incredibly supportive atmosphere for new unschoolers.[4]

The Social Life Question

One logistical unschooling question which I will address is the one that every unschooler gets asked at some point: How will you get a social life?

This question drives me crazy. It assumes that the only way to become socialized is in a classroom where you're forced to interact with other children by virtue of the fact that *they're the same age as you*. No other place in life does this idea emerge except compulsory schooling. If the concern is not about age, it is about race. Some people think that homeschoolers will become racists if they're not forced to sit next to people of different skin color every day. This is also backwards logic.

The real principle behind friendship and tolerance is this: people grow close through chosen activity, not shared captivity. Teens from diverse ages and backgrounds will bond when they're on the same soccer team, robotics club or working side-by-side in a business. In contrast, teens who are forced together with no common interests resort to judging each other by superficialities—thus creating the ruthless and shallow social environments found in most middle and high schools.[5]

Unschoolers can build rich social lives by firstly, keeping the friends they already have in high school, and secondly, making new friends (both young and old) through their self-chosen adventures.

Leaving school doesn't mean leaving your school friends. School only takes up the first half of the day: 7:00 AM–3:00 PM. The after school hours, 3:00 PM–10:00 PM, are still yours to spend with your school friends (blissfully unrestricted by classrooms, bells, 35-minute lunches and five-minute hall periods). After school extracurriculars like sports, music, groups and clubs don't disappear, either.

Even better social connections come through adventure. If you've ever been to summer camp, traveled abroad, started a band or worked on a group project out of interest, you know that friendships form fast and strong when you're faced with shared adventure. Any major unschooling adventure like volunteering, interning, crashing a college course or going to a conference or retreat will land you many potential friendships.

Additionally, learning to make friends for yourself as an unschooler is excellent preparation for college and beyond. High schoolers often find themselves stymied by the do-it-yourself challenge of socializing in the real world. Adventuring unschoolers, on the other hand, tend to have very active social lives thanks to their previous training in making friends in new and uncomfortable situations.

Unschooling doesn't mean sacrificing a social life. It's an opportunity to practice the real principle behind socializing: making friends through shared interests and activities.

The Portfolio

Finally, let's address the last big question in the unschooler's path to college: how will I actually apply? You already know which CP results you have to prove, and you've batched those results with steps from your dream map. You know what your target colleges are looking for. But what is the tool that will translate your unschooled accomplishments into a language that admissions officers can understand?

This tool is the portfolio: a comprehensive compilation of works documenting your college preparatory prowess.

According to the National Center for Home Education, 93% of colleges are willing to accept portfolios or course descriptions instead of a high school diploma.[6] So chances are good that your target schools will accept a portfolio as part of your application, but many schools don't state this publicly. To know if your target schools will definitely take a portfolio, use the instructions at the end of Chapter 2 to contact admission offices and get explicit permission.

What goes into a portfolio? A lot. The portfolio will be your power card for convincing colleges that you're a prepared student, so being thorough is essential. On the other hand, you also don't want to overwhelm anyone with a two-inch-thick bulging folder. To help you strike a balance in deciding what to including in the portfolio, I devised a handy acronym: SOUL PoWeR.

Standardized tests
Official transcript
Unofficial transcript
Letters of recommendation
Photographs
Writing sample
Résumé

The SOUL PoWeR portfolio hits every CP result that a college admissions officer wants to see. Here's how to build your own.

Standardized Tests

Scores from your SAT, ACT, AP, CLEP and other tests are sent by the testing agency directly to the colleges that you select on testing day.[7] Therefore, you don't have to actually include standardized test scores in your application. But I recommend including them anyway, primarily because standardized tests are a critical part of the unschooler's college application. Admissions people typically have little evidence of your logical reasoning capabilities, and seeing your test scores for a second time on paper will take the edge off. To include standardized test scores in your portfolio, simply print the scores and dates on their own sheet of paper.

Official Transcript

To show your structured learning results, include transcripts from any structured coursework that you've completed. This includes community college, distance coursework, summer seminars, audited college classes and any other graded work done in a structured academic environment. Include these *in addition* to the official transcripts that your college(s) require you to send directly, for the same reason that you included standardized test scores (reinforcement). Make photocopies of each transcript and stick them in the portfolio.

Unofficial Transcript

The bulk of your college preparatory activities are likely locked up (i.e., batched) inside your various unschooling adventures. To show how these adventures have academic merits, write your own unofficial transcript (a.k.a. homeschool transcript as described in chapter 2).[8] Unofficial transcripts smooth admission officers' feathers by speaking in a language that they understand: numbers. It may feel strange to call a month of back-to-back late-night writing sessions a half-unit of English, but this is how you will be heard.

To convert your activities into academic units, begin by estimating the number of hours that you spent on a particular activity over the course of a year. Round off numbers if need be, but don't be tempted to inflate your figures to make yourself look better. That policy will only hurt you in the end. If you spent *an average* of four hours practicing guitar for an average of three days a week for 20 weeks, then you can honestly say you spent 240 hours in Music this year. Next, divide your hour totals by 120 to yield the number of academic units for each class. In the above example, 240 hours of Music yielded two units for the year.

In case you're wondering, the units we're describing aren't arbitrary number choices. 120 hours constitutes the high school standard Carnegie unit, which has existed since 1906.[9] Admissions officers commonly use these units to analyze their high school applicants. Because Carnegie units don't include letter grades, you might consider creating your own grades (A, B, C, D, F) for your transcript. Most often, however, this isn't worth your time because colleges don't look at homeschool grades seriously. Grades are only useful indicators when they compare you to a large group of people.

Structure the transcript by breaking it into years or semesters, and list your activities in a format like this.

Sophomore Year

Acoustic Guitar and Music Theory, 2 Carnegie Units
- (accomplishments 1, 2 and 3)

Cognitive Science, ½ Carnegie Unit[10]
- (accomplishments 1, 2 and 3)

German Language, 1 Carnegie Unit
- (accomplishments 1, 2 and 3)

In the accomplishment bullet points, list the specific learning targets you met and the methods that used. Limit accomplishments to a maximum of three bullets points.

German Language, 1 Carnegie Unit

- Lived and worked on a family farm outside of Berlin, May 2008–July 2008 in German language immersion
- Worked with a language tutor two hours each week
- Read three untranslated major works of German fiction

Shannon Lee Clair, who entered Princeton as a freshman in 2005, also included under each of her academic units a list of books she had read, museums or sights that she had visited and relevant documentaries that she had watched.

Letters of Recommendation

In contrast to their high school peers, unschoolers typically develop in-depth relationships with numerous adults like intern supervisors, volunteer coordinators, working professionals and college graduate students. When asking yourself which adults will write you the best recommendation letters, chose those who have seen you overcome the biggest obstacles and challenges in your life. Because these adults are also likely very busy, make sure to ask for your letters at least two months before the due date.

Letters of recommendation are more important for homeschoolers than high schoolers because admissions people want to hear as much about your self-education story as possible. Here's what two previous case study schools have to say.

MIT

Extra recommendations can be especially helpful for many homeschooled applicants. We welcome a recommendation

> from a parent, but require at least three recommendations in total (usually a counselor and two teachers). We encourage you to submit additional recommendations (but don't submit more than 5 total recommendations) from those who know you well, such as coaches, mentors, job supervisors, clergy, etc.[11]

Stanford

> Typically, we require three evaluations: two from teachers of the student's choice and one from a guidance counselor or other school official. Your parents and/or your primary instructor(s) can write one evaluation in place of all three. While this evaluation is helpful in conveying in detail the context of your educational experience, it also lacks one crucial element: the objectivity brought by a conventional teacher able to compare one applicant with other students he or she may have taught. We do not expect parents to make such a comparison, but we do have to compare your credentials to thousands of others for whom we have an objective view. Teachers and guidance counselors can be biased, too, and this is why we ask for three letters, in the hope that each will independently verify and reinforce the others.[12]

As an example of the balance in recommendation letters that colleges want to see, Shannon Lee Clair used one letter from her community college French professor, one from a babysitting employer, one from the head of the theater where she interned for five months and one from a mother who ran a homeschooling Classics club. Shannon's community college professor likely provided the objectivity that Stanford described as desirable in homeschooling letters of recommendation; do your best to get at least one recommendation from a similarly established instructor.

Photographs

Photographs can be used to great advantage in a portfolio. An admissions officer might not believe that you spent two months at an arctic research station—until she sees photos of the dog sled team. Five good shots should do the trick. Use the 80/20 principle, as always; focus on impressive visual images. When printing your photos, use the highest-quality print service that you can find (photo printing websites typically offer excellent service for a low price). Nothing kills a good photo like an inkjet home printer.

Writing Sample

As with test scores and official transcripts, every college will require a written response as part of their application, but it is to your advantage as an unschooler to go above and beyond this requirement. Do this by including an *additional*, unsolicited writing sample in your portfolio.

Choose your best piece of writing—ideally, some sort of critical argument about a subject near your intended field of study. Keep it under three pages. And get the paper proofread by at least two English-savvy adults (because nothing kills a reader's confidance moore then bad spellng grammar and punctuatoin).

Résumé

Finally, to give admissions officers a birds-eye view of your life as a whole (including the non-batched and non-academic parts of your life that haven't yet made it into the portfolio), create a résumé.

Begin by seeking out résumé-writing advice, which abounds both online and in books. Virtually all of this advice will be directed toward adults seeking full-time employment, but the principles can typically be applied to your unschooling adventures. Instead of the categories Formal Education or Work Experience, you might create your own categories like Travel, Internships, Self-Study or Martial Arts.

A well-written résumé will synthesize the disparate parts of your life into a compelling narrative in chronological order. When an admissions officer puts it down, he should be thinking, I wish I had been doing that when I was in high school!

The Cover Letter

This last touch isn't part of our handy SOUL PoWeR acronym, I know. But it is the ribbon that seals the package.

Faced with a beautiful binder full of your transcripts, photographs, test scores, essays, letters of recommendation and résumé, an admissions officer unfamiliar with unschooling may be overwhelmed. Take his hand and guide him through your masterpiece with the help of a cover letter.

A traditional cover letter is a one-two page paper in which you briefly describe your motivation and background for the job to which you're applying. In this case, the job is college, and your cover letter should describe

1. your personal educational philosophy, what made you choose it and how it has evolved with time and experience.
2. why you want to go to college, what you plan to accomplish there and what you have to offer to the college community.
3. the steps you took to prepare for college.
4. how the materials inside this portfolio prove your college readiness (the five CP results).

Position the cover letter so that it is the first thing that the admission officer will see upon opening your package.

Sending It In

With your portfolio ready, consult individual colleges on how they want it delivered. Often you'll simply stick your portfolio materials in the same oversized envelope as your application.

The rest of the college application process is easily found on college websites: print the application, answer the writing prompts, forward your official transcripts and test scores and mail it all before the winter deadline.

And that's it. Congratulations! College without high school.

The Life Unschool

What, in the end, is the point of unschooling? Allow me to wax poetic for a moment.

Unschooling is more than a tactic for teenage adventure and independent college prep. It is a personal philosophic revolution.

To unschool is to affirm that life is worth living. When you leave school to educate yourself on your own terms, you're declaring that

- **there is good and joy to be found in the world,**
- **pursuing your joy is your fundamental right,**
- **and you are not afraid to uphold that right.**

Unschooling embraces the individual's right to own her life and to make what she will of it. It is a philosophy of self-determination and self-empowerment. It denies any form of social predestination or caste system. You are the purpose of your life, and only you will make your life great.

The opposite of unschooling is the attitude of a broken high school student. It is the belief that happiness cannot be found in life, that others will always control your affairs and that attempts in self-improvement are futile. You are born weak, and you will stay weak. The purpose of your life, if any, is eternal self-sacrifice to some greater good, whether it be god, government or society.

The difference between these two outlooks is a choice. When you choose to unschool, you choose to become an actor in life instead of a pawn.

Monica Chen found her reason to unschool in Emerson's words: "We are always getting ready to live, but never living." My inspiration came from John Gatto's words, which drove me as a college student (too far down the path of institutional schooling) to affirm that my dreams were worth living. Words are powerful weapons, and my hope is that the words in this book have inspired you to take your own life and pursuit of joy more seriously.

John Gatto once gave a commencement address to a group of graduating homeschoolers and passed along a singular piece of advice.

> The only thing serious you face at the moment, regardless of what you've been told, is deciding what quests you will choose for yourself.[1]

Now it's time for you to begin your quests. Unschooling is only a metaphor for life unleashed at full volume. Enjoy the ride.

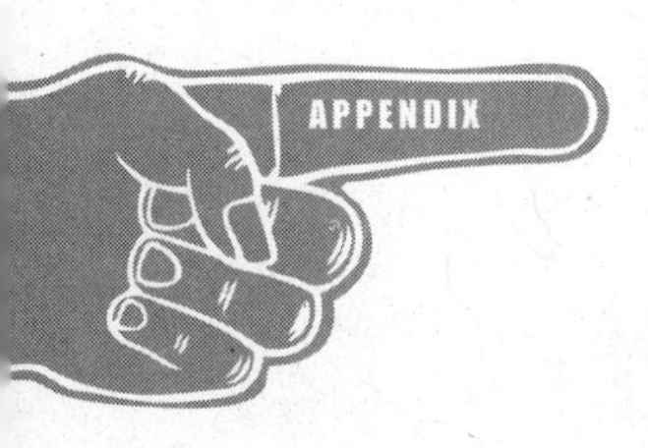

Uncollege

This book's mission is to help you define your dreams, get an education that doesn't bore you to tears and do college prep on your own terms—as a teen. But what if the unschooling revolution hits you and you're already in college? Is there a way to unschool college?

There is indeed. If your college experience needs a boost of excitement, challenge or personalization, then don't just follow along with your major's curriculum—make college work for you. The art of doing this I call uncolleging.

We will discuss the following uncolleging tactics.

- Skipping boring or unproductive classes
- Custom-designing a major to fit specific interests and goals
- Taking professors to lunch, chatting up graduate students and seeking advice from seniors as a freshmen
- Exploiting Pass/No Pass, independent study and thesis options
- Joining high-level research projects
- Interning, volunteering and studying abroad
- Teaching a course to other undergrads

Each of these tactics will help you make full use of the personal freedom and tremendous learning resources that a four-year college provides.

Skip Unproductive Classes

If a college course stinks, just skip it. You'll run into a few such classes on your way toward any major. Get a friend to deliver homework assignments (or find them online), show up for mid-terms and finals and learn on your own.

I wouldn't state this seemingly obvious tactic if I hadn't seen so many UC Berkeley students sit through hours of mind-numbing lectures (most often in the maths and sciences) where the professor essentially read from the textbook. Auditory learners benefited, perhaps, from this rote lecture, but the majority of students sat there because they thought attendance was mandatory. It wasn't.

Lower-division, lecture-heavy classes with 100+ students rarely give grades for attendance. The chore of taking role is simply too big for the teaching assistants. If a class does require lecture attendance, you'll find out in the first class or the course paperwork. The vast majority of classes provide lectures for your optional benefit only.

What is the alternative to learning via lecture? Some students can learn directly from the textbook. For the rest of us, let's first ask what a lecture is supposed to accomplish. Ideally a lecture walks you step-by-step through the logical train of a subject, pausing to answer common questions and illustrate difficult ideas along the way. You can reproduce this on your own schedule.

- Download the lecture via webcast (if available) and fast-forward to specific parts.
- Find web tutorials on specific subjects (if written by graduate students, they tend to have excellent quality).
- Join or organize a study group with other students.
- Supplement the textbook with higher-quality books, e.g. the Feynman Lectures on Physics for introductory physics.

- Use professor and graduate student office hours (discussed in more detail below).

Unlike lectures, weekly class discussion sections (one-two hours) are typically mandatory. Go to these.

Custom-Design a Major

I kicked off my uncolleging life by designing my own major, and it was the best thing that I ever did for my education. Major design is more of an option for liberal art and soft science majors (like literature, history, political science, psychology and art). The hard sciences (like math and engineering) typically have rigid curricula that make self-design difficult.

At UC Berkeley, I wanted to combine two years of math and hard science (my astrophysics background) with a future two years of alternative education history, philosophy and pedagogy. The IDS (Interdepartmental Studies) department initially gave me bad news: they only customize majors by crossing one liberal art with another—not a liberal art with a hard science. And per departmental requirements, they would also require me to take an additional three mysterious Interdisciplinary Study classes. No thank you! Don't give up at the first gatekeeper.

After a week of pushing, probing and generally making myself a nuisance, an IDS secretary tipped me off to the program that I was looking for: the Independent Major. This unpublished program, which enrolled seven students out of Berkeley's 20,000 undergraduates, let students design a major from scratch. The program's office was an IDS advisor's file cabinet. I walked into this advisor's office and, after asking how I found her (!), she told me what I needed to draft for the Independent Major: a proposal letter and a course list. Additionally, I would need two Berkeley professors to sign off as my advisors and eventually grade my required senior thesis paper. Within three weeks I researched and wrote my proposal and course list, had them signed off by two favorite professors and filed to officially change from Astrophysics to the Independent Major. The whole process took no more than two months.

You can discover your own major design options by searching your school's website or walking into the office of the Interdisciplinary Studies, Interdepartmental Studies or similar department. What you're looking for may be a hidden sub-department; ask around and don't be afraid to approach deans, chairs, provosts or any of the other esoteric officers of your college who may hold the key to your success.

Take Professors to Lunch, Chat up Graduate Students and Seek Advice from Seniors as a Freshman

The vast majority of college students don't talk to their professors or graduate student instructors outside of lecture and discussion sections. This makes competition for one-on-one time with these potential mentors incredibly low. An uncolleger uses this fact to go straight to the intellectual heart of college by tracking down professors, grad students and experienced older students for guidance, inspiration and insight.

Apply the same tactics described in Chapter 4's Hunting Down Heroes and Experts section to your uncollege hunt.

1. Start with dream map questions.
2. Do your homework (investigate targets' accomplishments and research interests).
3. Walk into the office (you're an enrolled student, after all — no need for cautionary e-mails or phone calls).
4. Be brief (30 minutes max).
5. Ask for follow-up e-mail permissions.
6. Actually follow-up within one week.

It may take change of scenery to get your grad student or professor to be open for a real conversation; to that end, take them out for coffee. College towns are loaded with coffee shops, and a $4 latte is unquestionably worth an hour of picking a particle physicist's brain.

If you're a freshman, find a senior in your intended field of study to act as an informal mentor. Smart seniors often hang out with grad students and professors, and you can meet them at department colloquia (these are also good places to meet graduate students and professors). Colloquia are one- to two-hour presentations given by local or visiting researchers, typically followed by a snacking-and-socializing event. Look for the person who looks youngest in the room (most likely to be an undergraduate), introduce yourself and ask about her research interests. Ask who the best and worst lecturing professors are, ask why she chose this field and what she intends to do after graduating. And once you've got the ball rolling, you can pop the question: can I have your e-mail address to ask you more questions about this major?

Exploit Pass/No Pass, Independent Study and Thesis Options

In all but the most rigid majors, you have a wide variety of elective options. Want to learn about ecology as an English major? No problem. Spanish as a Statistics major? It can be done. But elective classes that you take out of interest—not as a part of your major program—are less fun with the looming threat of a bad grade. The solution is to take these courses ungraded, a.k.a. pass/no pass or pass/fail. Often you can take up to ¼ or ⅓ of your total units as pass/no pass.

Independent study and senior thesis courses are two options for doing serious self-designed work in college, and they also give you units in your major field. They typically require only a sponsoring professor and a written proposal on your part. Ask your major advisor about doing either, because often these opportunities go unpublicized.

Join High-level Research Projects

The distinguishing factor between universities and colleges is where on the totem pole a school places research (of the high-brow academic variety). At a university, professors are researchers first and teachers second; at a college, they are teachers first, researchers second. And in community college, teachers are typically only teachers.

If you're a university student, at some point without fail you'll hear this line: "This professor stinks. They don't care about teaching here, just doing research." And chances are good indeed that you'll run into university professors who indeed are terrible lecturers—but prolific researchers. Don't moan. When life hands you researchers, make research.

Research is the cutting edge of academia where intellectual breakthroughs are made and papers are published. Researchers work in groups, typically one or more professors with a handful of graduate students. These groups will have two needs: inducting new talent into their circle and finding free help with field research, data crunching and other time-intensive activities. This is where you, the undergraduate research assistant, fit in.

You have two options for getting your hands dirty in a real-life, high-level research project: the front door and the back door.

The front door is university-sponsored undergraduate research programs. These programs will match you up with a research project of interest and take care of the paperwork. Search your university's website for its undergrad research program and see what they offer. The potential downsides of the university-sponsored program are competition, red tape and the fact that not every research group registers with the undergrad research program.

The back door is the uncollege door. Find a particular research project that fascinates you and show up at one of its grad student's offices. Say that you'd like to make yourself useful. And if they don't have a place for you at first, offer to get coffee or make photocopies.

Getting your foot into a high-level research group is like getting an internship at a desirable enterprise: because you're new and untested, you'll have to first prove that you're dedicated to the project. No self-respecting research team will let you get coffee and make photocopies for a year. They'll take pity and start giving you real research tasks. And then you can begin to make yourself indispensable, and the biggest research opportunities will follow.

Intern, Volunteer, Work and Study Abroad

Opportunities for interning, volunteering, working and studying abroad abound in college. You can spend a semester in Patagonia, volunteer in Costa Rica or apprentice as a stagehand for a summer. When sponsored by your college, adventures like these can be financed by your financial aid.

My friend David found a particularly valuable internship opportunity during his undergraduate years. David studied engineering at Northwestern University under a university-sponsored co-op program with Caterpillar (a.k.a. CAT, the company that makes the giant yellow construction vehicles). He alternated between semesters of academics at Northwestern and paid internship work at the CAT headquarters in Peoria, an hour away. David's dream is to build an ultra-efficient, clean-burning car engine; the co-op program gave him the real-world experience necessary to jump straight into his desired field after graduating.

Teach a Course to Other Undergrads

Finally, the grandest uncollege tactic (and perhaps the most challenging) is designing and leading your own college course in which other undergraduates will enroll for real credit. Self-initiated courses fit the uncolleger personality perfectly. Designing your own course demands a passion and deep knowledge of your subject, a willingness to confront professors and college administrators and a desire to share your insight with others. The savvy uncolleger, by junior or senior year, is highly qualified for the job.

Starting your own course requires a lot of paperwork and hoop-jumping, but the payoff is worth it. In 2003 I created a course on critical education theory called Never Taught to Learn with a friend. The following semester I led the course myself, followed by a short personality typing course. Each of these courses forced me to learn more about my subject than I would have in self-study.

The most difficult part of starting your own course is having the framework for it in the first place—only a handful of colleges have student-run course programs. But these colleges can help you start a similar program at your own school. Search online for SIC at Stanford, the Experimental College at Tufts and Oberlin, USIE at UCLA. The oldest and best program to consult is DeCal at my own alma mater, UC Berkeley.[1]

If you can pull it off, teaching your own class will be grandest college adventure possible.

Reading and Resources

The following books and websites informed and inspired the ideas in this book.

The Big Two

Grace Llewellyn. *The Teenage Liberation Handbook: How to Quit School and Get a Real Life and Education.* Lowry House, 1998.
Grace kicked off an unschooling revolution by gifting a small movement with a giant inspirational jolt. Written directly for teens (like this book), the *TLH* covers every aspect of unschooling from convincing parents, to teaching yourself history, to finding mentorships, internships and other adventures. Packed with stories about real-life unschooling teens, this is a must-have for every prospective unschooler.

John Taylor Gatto. *Weapons of Mass Instruction: A Schoolteacher's Journey through the Dark World of Compulsory Schooling.* New Society, 2008.
John Gatto taught in NYC public schools for 30 years, became Teacher of the Year in both New York City and New York State, quit his job (so he would no longer have to "hurt kids to make a living"), and began writing and lecturing widely on the history of compulsory schooling. Don't let his complex theses scare you away from his genius solutions to the problem of growing up in an absurd educational system.

More Top Choices

John Holt and Patrick Farenga. *Teach Your Own: The John Holt Book of Homeschooling.* De Capo, 2003.
A primer for homeschooling and self-directed learning, written by the founding father of unschooling.

Grace Llewellyn. *Real Lives: Eleven Teenagers Who Don't Go to School Tell Their Own Stories.* Lowry House, 2005.
In-depth accounts of eleven teenage unschoolers, including follow-up interviews from nearly a decade later.

John Taylor Gatto. *The Underground History of American Education: A School Teacher's Intimate Investigation Into the Problem of Modern Schooling. 2nd ed.* Oxford Village Press, 2001.
Gatto's *magnum opus* is a thick but incredibly rewarding read that properly dashes the lingering, unfounded hopes for school reform that keep many families from attempting real alternatives in education.[1]

John Taylor Gatto. *Dumbing Us Down: The Hidden Curriculum of Compulsory Schooling.* New Society, 2002.
John Taylor Gatto. *A Different Kind of Teacher: Solving the Crisis of American Schooling.* Berkeley Hills, 2001.
These are also excellent introductions to Gatto's ideas; the latter book was the one that kicked off my own uncolleging career.

Self-Directed Education Centers

Daniel Greenberg. *The Sudbury Valley School Experience.* Sudbury Valley School, 1992.
Of the dozens of books printed by Sudbury Valley, this is the best for an bird's eye view of the school's compelling philosophy.

A.S. Neill. ed. Albert Lamb. *Summerhill School: A New View of Childhood.* St. Martin's Griffin, 1995.
The original free school, founded in England.

North Star: Self-Directed Learning for Teens website [online]. [cited March 23, 2009]. northstarteens.org.
Formed by two former public school teachers in central Massachusetts, North Star offers unschooling in a school format with daily optional classes and personal mentoring.

Not Back to School Camp website. [online]. [cited March 23, 2009]. nbtsc .org.
Week-long gatherings for unschooled teens held during the time of year when other teens go back to school. Not to be missed.

College Admissions

Donald Asher. *Cool Colleges: For the Hyper-Intelligent, Self-Directed, Late Blooming, and Just Plain Different. 2nd ed.* Ten Speed, 2007.
Helpful for researching colleges that fit the unschooling mindset a bit better than your local state college.

Cafi Cohen. *And What About College? How Homeschooling Leads to Admissions to the Best Colleges and Universities.* Holt Associates, 2000.
A comprehensive narrative of the homeschool-to-college process.

Loretta Heuer. *Homeschooler's Guide to Portfolios and Transcripts.* Arco, 2000.
An overwhelming number of ideas of for designing and organizing your portfolio and unschool transcript.

Learn in Freedom. Colleges That Admit Homeschoolers FAQ. [online]. [cited March 23,2009]. learninfreedom.org/colleges_4_hmsc.html.
Lists every college to which a homeschooler has been admitted.

Post-College

Michael Landes. *The Back Door Guide to Short-Term Job Adventures: Internships, Summer Jobs, Seasonal Work, Volunteer Vacations, and Transitions Abroad.* Ten Speed, 2005.
All the cool jobs you never knew existed. Mostly for ages 18+.

Timothy Ferriss. *The 4-Hour Workweek: Escape 9–5, Live Anywhere, and Join the New Rich.* Crown, 2007.
Written for corporate cubicle refugees seeking both more adventure and more money in their lives. Ferriss is a master of leveraged risk-taking, batching, entrepreneurship and goal-setting, and he heavily inspired my writings on those same topics in this book.

Online Learning Resources

Any list of online resources is destined for quick obsolescence. Use these links as leads for further research!

SparkNotes website. [online]. [cited March 23, 2009]. sparknotes.com

UC Berkeley Video and Podcasts for Courses and Events [online], [cited March 23, 2009]. webcast.berkeley.edu.

MIT OpenCourseWare. [online]. [cited March 23, 2009]. ocw.mit.edu/OcwWeb/web/home/home/index.htm

Princeton University Webmedia. [online]. [cited March 23, 2009]. princeton.edu/WebMedia.

UCLA Office of Instructional Development. [online]. [cited March 23, 2009]. oid.ucla.edu/webcasts.

Acknowledgments

My first thanks go to Nathaniel Singer, who inspired my college turn-around by handing me a John Gatto book bought on his own dime. The next thanks go to the UC Berkeley professors and staff who made my individual major possible — especially Geoff Marcy, astronomy professor extraordinaire and enthusiastic supporter of my clumsy senior thesis paper.

Many thanks and banished T'NACI monsters to Jim Wiltens and the instructors and campers of Deer Crossing Summer Camp. You showed me the meaning of hard work, self-reliance, attitude and creativity.

Grace Llewellyn and the staff and campers of Not Back to School Camp welcomed an outsider with open arms and gave me the raw inspiration that I needed to turn a scrawl of notes into a cohesive whole. You have created an incredibly special camp in a small patch of the Oregon and Vermont woods. May it last forever.

Charlotte Wagoner, Keren Zucker, Andy Pearson, Jenny Bowen, Shannon Lee Clair, Emerie Snyder, Jason Crawford, Siobhan Moore, Monica Chen, Dave Thomas and Brenna McBroom: thank you for sharing the stories that breathed life into this book.

I am thoroughly indebted to Grace Llewellyn, Nathaniel Singer, Ken Danford and Gia Albaum for the feedback they provided on my first draft. Grace, you especially provided the in-depth punches to the gut that I needed to form my writing into a logical and balanced final product. Silvia Killingsworth showed no mercy with grammar and punctuation as my proofreader, and Virginia Berger-Hawthorne patiently tackled my graphic design problems. Ingrid Witvoet, EJ Hurst, Sue Custance and the rest of the New Society team coached me through the publishing process with gusto and aplomb, and Betsy Nuse made copy editing feel like a back rub.

Finally, thank you Dad for always holding my writing and ideas to the highest intellectual standard. And thank you Mom for your unwavering support in each of my projects.

Endnotes

Through the Macroscope

1. A Public Ivy (a term coined by Richard Mill) is a public college or university that provides an Ivy League collegiate experience at a public school price.
2. John Taylor Gatto. *A Different Kind of Teacher: Solving the Crisis in American Schooling.* Berkeley Hills, 2001, p. 15 .

A Note for Parents

1. John Taylor Gatto. *Weapons of Mass Instruction.* New Society, 2008, pp. 32–33.

Chapter 1: Redefining Teen

1. If you're 16 or 17 and plan to enroll full-time in community college, you may be able to legally leave high school without declaring yourself a homeschooler. Check with your local community college.
2. The term unschooling was first used by educator John Holt.
3. See Paula Polk Lillard. *Montessori Today: A Comprehensive Approach to Education from Birth to Adulthood.* Schocken, 1996 and Maria Montessori. From *Childhood to Adolescence: Including Erdkinder and the Function of the University.* ABC-CLIO, 1994.
4. Adapted from Grace Llewellyn, *The Teenage Liberation Handbook: How to Quit School and Get a Real Life and Education.* Revised edition. Lowry House, 1998, p. 371. For further research, find the Forbes list of world billionaires and read each member's educational background.
5. Martha Rainbolt and Janet Fleetwood. *On the Contrary: Essays by Men and Women.* SUNY Press, 1983, p. 133.
6. Walter Isaacson. *Einstein: His Life and Universe.* Illustrated edition. Simon & Schuster, 2007, p. 49.

7. An especially worthwhile book for unschoolers seeking colleges is Donald Asher. *Cool Colleges: for the Hyper-Intelligent, Self-Directed, Late Blooming, and Just Plain Different.* 2nd edition. Ten Speed, 2007.
8. These goal-setting strategies inspired by James S. Wiltens. *Goal Express.* Deer Crossing, 1995 and Timothy Ferriss. *The 4-Hour Workweek: Escape 9–5, Live Anywhere, and Join the New Rich.* Crown, 2007.
9. To see John Goddard's full list of goals (and the new ones he writes every year), see Official Website of John Goddard. My Life List. [online]. [cited March 10, 2009]. johngoddard.info/life_list.htm.

Chapter 2: College Prep Without School

1. National Center for Education Statistics. Homeschooling in the United States: 2003. [online]. [cited March 11, 2009]. US Department of Education, Institute of Education Sciences, publication NCES 2006–042, p. 1.
2. Don Dunbar and G.F. Lichtenberg. *What You Don't Know Can Keep You Out of College: A Top Consultant Explains the 13 Fatal Application Mistakes and Why Character Is the Key to College Admissions.* Gotham, 2007.
3. Partially adapted from Shannon Lee Clair. "Looking Back After A Year of College, Part 2." [online]. [Cited March 11, 2009]. LINK Homeschool News Network Vol. 9 #2. homeschoolnewslink.com/homeschool/articles/vol9iss2/v9i2_lookingback2.shtml.
4. Michelle Conlin. "Smashing the Clock." *BusinessWeek,* December 11 2006. [online]. [cited March 12, 2009]. businessweek.com/magazine/content/06_50/b4013001.htm. As far as I can determine, Best Buy's current (2009) financial woes are not a direct result of ROWE.
5. With determination, you can get around an SAT/ACT requirement. See the story of Amanda Bergon-Shilcock, a University of Pennsylvania graduate, in Grace Llewellyn. *Real Lives: Eleven Teenagers Who Don't Go to School Tell Their Own Stories.* Lowry House, 2005.
6. More competitive colleges have higher standards in granting credits for these tests. For example, one school may accept a score of 3 on a certain AP exam, and another will only accept a 5 (the highest score). Check with your schools for AP and CLEP credit-granting policies.
7. The Massachusetts Institute of Technology (MIT) is a top math, science and engineering university in the Boston area; Stanford is a top liberal arts university in the San Francisco Bay area; the University of California at Riverside is a moderately competitive public research university

in Southern California. To browse more colleges with online admissions policies for homeschoolers, visit A to Z Home's Cool Homeschooling. Colleges with Homeschool Admission Policies Online. [online]. [cited March 12, 2009]. homeschooling.gomilpitas.com/olderkids/CollegeHS pages.htm.

8. MIT. Homeschooled Applicants: Helpful Tips. [online]. [cited March 12, 2009]. mitadmissions.org/topics/apply/homeschooled_applicants_helpful_tips/.
9. Stanford University Undergraduate Admission Application Requirements. Home-Schooled Applicant Guidelines. [online]. [cited March 12, 2009]. stanford.edu/dept/uga/basics/requirements/home_school.html.
10. My UCR—Paths to Admission. Admission as a Homeschooled or Other Nontraditionally Educated Student. [online]. [cited March 12, 2009]. my.ucr.edu/admissions/paths.aspx.

Chapter 3: The Six-Hour School Week

1. See "And 'Rithmetic" in Daniel Greenberg, ed. *Free at Last: The Sudbury Valley School.* Sudbury Valley School Press, 1995, pp. 15–18.
2. See Daniel Greenberg and Mimsy Sadofsky. *Legacy of Trust: Life After the Sudbury Valley School Experience.* Sudbury Valley School Press, 1992.
3. We consider the freshman, sophomore and junior years of high school—the bulk of the college preparatory period.

Chapter 4: The Adventure Blender

1. Remembering someone's name is a mark of professionalism. Write the names of people you meet during phone calls and in face-to-face meetings on a piece of paper and use their names often.
2. Gatekeepers are the employees who stand between you and the people, like owners or human resources managers, who can actually give you an internship. The first person you speak with is most likely a gatekeeper. Be courteous, but remember that the gatekeeper is not your goal. Get transferred to someone higher up as soon as possible.
3. Be prepared to use synonyms for the word internship at first. Volunteering or job shadowing may get you past the gatekeeper when internship doesn't.
4. Homeschooler is a better choice than unschooler (or other esoteric labels) for introductions.

5. Answering this question without hesitation (using your list of internship goals) will build major rapport with your interviewer.
6. Reinforce that your intention is to serve—not to pick and choose between tasks depending on your mood.
7. The Center for Interim Programs, LLC website. [online]. [cited March 18, 2009]. interimprograms.com.
8. Volunteer Latin America website. [online]. [cited March 18, 2009]. volunteerlatinamerica.com.
9. Skype. "Make free calls and set your conversations free with Skype." [online]. [cited March 18, 2009]. skype.com.
10. US Department of State. Bureau of Consular Affairs. [online]. [cited March 18, 2009]. travel.state.gov.
11. *The Teenage Liberation Handbook*, p. 341.
12. Craigslist, Inc. website. [online]. [cited March 19, 2009]. craigslist.org/about/sites.
13. Vistaprint US website. [online]. [cited March 19, 2009]. vistaprint.com.

Chapter 5: Making the Leap

1. Timothy Ferriss. *The 4-Hour Workweek: Escape 9–5, Live Anywhere, and Join the New Rich.* Crown, 2007, p. 40.
2. According to Grace, the next edition of the TLH will not include an updated legal section. Because regulations change so often, she recommends using the Internet to figure out your state's homeschooling laws.
3. You can get yourself a copy via the publisher's website: Lowry House. The Teenage Liberration Handbook. [online]. [cited March 19, 2009]. lowryhousepublishers.com/TeenageLiberationHandbook.htm.
4. Not Back to School Camp website. [online]. [cited March 19, 2009]. nbtsc.org.
5. For illuminating responses to the typical attacks against unschooling on the basis of socialization, see John Holt and Patrick Farenga. *Teach Your Own: The John Holt Book of Homeschooling.* DaCapo, 2003, chapter 2.
6. Christopher J. Klicka. *Home Students Excel in College.* Rev. ed. National Center for Home Education, 1998, p. 1, cited in Susan Wise and Jessie Bauer. *The Well-Trained Mind: A Guide to Classical Education at Home.* Norton, 2004, p. 688.
7. If you take a test early and decide later to apply to different colleges,

you'll need to pay the College Board a small fee to send scores to those new schools.

8. For in-depth discussion of building homeschool transcripts, see books by Cafi Cohen and Loretta Heuer in the Reading and Resources section.
9. The Carnegie Foundation FAQs. What is the Carnegie Unit? [online]. [cited March 19, 2009]. carnegiefoundation.org/about/sub.asp?key=17&subkey=1874.
10. Round Carnegie Units to the nearest ½ unit (nearest 60 hours).
11. MIT Admissions. Homeschooled Applicants—Helpful Tips. [online]. [cited March 20, 2009]. mitadmissions.org/topics/apply/homeschooled_applicants_helpful_tips/
12. Stanford University. Home-Schooled Applicant Guidelines. [online]. [cited March 20, 2009]. stanford.edu/dept/uga/basics/requirements/home_school.html.

Afterword: The Life Unschool

1. John Taylor Gatto. *The Awful Fate of Being Nobody; How To Avoid It.* A Commencement Address for Homeschoolers. 2005. [online]. [cited March 20, 2009]. homeschoolnewslink.com/homeschool/columnists/gatto/v7i6_fate_nobody.shtml.

Appendix: Uncollege

1. DeCal. Democratic Education at Cal. [online]. [cited March 20, 2009]. decal.org

Reading and Resources

1. You can find this book on the author's website: The Odysseus Group/John Taylor Gatto. Books, CDs, Audio and Video Cassettes. [online]. [cited March 30, 2009]. johntaylorgatto.com/bookstore/index.htm.

Index

About the Author

Blake Boles realized halfway through an astrophysics major that school and education are not the same thing. Blake is the co-founder of Unschool Adventures (unschooladventures.com), a company that leads innovative trips for self-directed teens. He is the former acting director of Deer Crossing Summer Camp, an advisor to unschooled teens at Not Back to School Camp, a Wilderness Emergency Medical Technician and a UC Berkeley graduate.

Ryan Brennan

blakeboles.com

New Society Publishers

ENVIRONMENTAL BENEFITS STATEMENT

New Society Publishers has chosen to produce this book on recycled paper made with 100% post consumer waste, processed chlorine free, and old growth free.

For every 5,000 books printed, New Society saves the following resources:[1]

16	Trees
1,462	Pounds of Solid Waste
1,609	Gallons of Water
2,098	Kilowatt Hours of Electricity
2,658	Pounds of Greenhouse Gases
11	Pounds of HAPs, VOCs, and AOX Combined
4	Cubic Yards of Landfill Space

[1] Environmental benefits are calculated based on research done by the Environmental Defense Fund and other members of the Paper Task Force who study the environmental impacts of the paper industry.

NEW SOCIETY PUBLISHERS